JERYAKEUI YEC
©Cho Yongho, 2024
Originally published in Korea by Wisely (Books)

The Queen of Strategy
©Cho Yongho, 2024

First English edition, first printing, published on November 15, 2024
Author: Cho Yongho
Editor: Cheon Jinsook
Cover Design: Cheon Jinsook
Published by: Cho Yongho
Publisher: Wisely
Publication Registration No. 385-251002021000003 (January 21, 2021)
Phone: 82-2-3454-1108
Fax: 82-50-4271-5046
Email: brad.cho@thebook.center
Website: http://thebook.center

ISBN 979-11-989362-2-6
Price is listed on the back cover.

The author and Wisely reserve all rights of this book.
Reproduction of any part or this entire book requires written consent from both parties.

The Queen of Strategy

The Struggles of New Manager Minji in Reviving a Company

Written by Cho Yongho

Wisely

thebook.center

Character Introduction

Seo Minji
- Age 28, starting as a new assistant manager at Hankook Electronics, quickly rises through the ranks
- Possesses excellent analytical skills and creative problem-solving abilities
- Fearless in the face of challenges, constantly learning and growing
- Overcomes the company's crises through strategic thinking and leadership

Chairman Kim
- Late 60s, Chairman of Hankook Electronics
- Leads the company with extensive experience and insight
- Recognizes the need for change and sees potential in Minji
- Sometimes strict but open to innovative ideas

Kang Hyunwoo

- Mid-40s, external strategy consultant and Minji's mentor
- Provides Minji with advice based on his wealth of experience and knowledge
- Combines cold analytical skills with warm human qualities
- Helps Minji grow and offers insightful advice at crucial moments

Na Minho

- Age 35, Head of Strategy at Mirae Electronics and Minji's rival
- A brilliant strategist and Hankook Electronics' biggest competitor
- Cold and calculating but sometimes acts unpredictably
- Pushes Minji to grow through competition

Park Sungjun

- Age 45, Head of Human Resources at Hankook Electronics
- Fair and methodical, excellent in organizational management

- Initially skeptical of Minji's rapid promotion, but gradually recognizes and supports her abilities

Kim Seojin
- Age 32, Manager in Hankook Electronics' Marketing Team
- Creative and passionate, forms a strong team dynamic with Minji
- Provides key insights into Minji's strategies with a customer-centric approach

Lee Jooyoung
- Age 26, Researcher at Hankook Electronics
- Contributes to Minji's strategy execution with his outstanding technical skills and innovative ideas
- Represents the younger generation's perspective and sometimes challenges existing norms

Synopsis of 'The Queen of Strategy'-New Manager Minji's Journey to Reviving the Company

Episode 1: Realizing the Need for Change

New Assistant Manager Seo Minji joins Hankook Electronics. She identifies the company's crisis caused by Mirae Electronics' innovative smart home system launch. She presents a bold proposal to the executives and they appoint her as the leader of a new strategic task force.

Episode 2: A Bird's-eye View

Mirae Electronics announces an AI-based smart home platform dominating the market. Minji formulates a counterstrategy using PEST analysis and Porter's Five Forces model, but the executives reject her proposal in a meeting. With advice from external coach Kang Hyunwoo, she overcomes the crisis through a novel approach.

Episode 3: Omija Princess and the Convenience Store

Jooyoung spends a weekend at a neighborhood convenience store for a meal, reminiscing about a pivotal moment from her past in graduate school.

Episode 4: Capturing the Customer's Heart
Mirae Electronics launches a new AI-based product. To find a breakthrough, Minji conducts customer segmentation and customer journey mapping. She discovers hidden market needs and proposes a new product launch, earning a promotion to manager.

Episode 5: Shimpyo, A New Beginning
Minji learns about the financial struggles of her favorite cafe near Hongdae and offers help. The cafe rebrands with a new concept and successfully revives, becoming a local hotspot.

Episode 6: Finding Answers Within
Mirae Electronics begins aggressively scouting Hankook Electronics' top talent with attractive offers. Minji conducts SWOT analysis and value chain analysis to rediscover the company's strengths. Collaborating with the HR team, she develops a new talent development program that successfully retains key personnel.

Episode 7: Chairman Kim's Mountain Lesson

During a brief weekend hike near his home, Chairman Kim realizes that Hankook Electronics stands at a crossroads and decides to push for changes to move the company forward.

Episode 8: Moving Towards One Direction

Chairman Kim sets out to establish a new vision for the company's future. Minji, tasked with leading a company-wide workshop to define Hankook Electronics' new vision and mission, uses a strategy map to present a compelling future plan amid internal conflicts. Her achievements lead to her promotion as a senior manager.

Episode 9: The Crisis of 'Happy Flower Shop'

Hyunwoo notices a local flower shop he frequents during holidays is struggling. Unable to ignore its plight, he helps the shop overcome structural challenges, ultimately leading to its successful transformation.

Episode 10: The Innovation Battle

Mirae Electronics releases a groundbreaking integrated AI smart home system. In response, Minji uses a business model canvas to design a new business model and leads the rapid development of an MVP. She overcomes internal resistance with a fresh approach and successfully launches an innovative service.

Episode 11: The Strategist and the North Star

As Na Minho's contract with Mirae Electronics nears its end, he contemplates his next steps. During a chance encounter with Minji, he finds a clue for his future direction.

Episode 12: The Challenge of Uncharted Territory

Chairman Kim instructs Minji to explore new markets with no competition. She and her team identify a new business area and launch an innovative product targeting previously overlooked customer segments.

Episode 13: Facing Inner Change

After running nonstop, Minji takes a short sabbatical and plans to travel abroad. Before departing, she meets with her coach to reflect on the challenges she has faced and the solutions she found, using these moments as steppingstones for her future growth.

Table of Contents

Episode 1: Realizing the Need for Change — 13
Episode 2: Surveying with a Bird's-eye View — 33
Episode 3: The Omija Princess and the Convenience Store — 45
Episode 4: Capturing the Customer's Heart — 62
Episode 5: Shimpyo, A New Beginning — 78
Episode 6: Finding the Answers Within — 94
Episode 7: Chairman Kim's Mountain Lesson — 115
Episode 8: Moving in One Direction — 125
Episode 9: The Crisis of 'Happy Flower Shop' — 145
Episode 10: The Battle of Innovation — 176
Episode 11: The Strategist and the North Star — 201
Episode 12: A Leap into the Unknown — 218
Episode 13: Facing the Change Within — 237
Epilogue — 248

Episode 1: Realizing the Need for Change

In front of the Hankook Electronics headquarters, Seo Minji took a deep breath. Today was her first day at this new company, her second job. On this bright spring morning, hope and passion enveloped her eyes, yet there was also a hint of anxiety. "It's finally starting," Minji thought to herself. "I will grow with this company and make it to the top."

As she entered the lobby, a grand exhibition hall greeted her. On display were products representing the 70-year history of Hankook Electronics, from black-and-white TVs to the latest smart appliances, all showing the company's evolution. Guided to her desk by an HR employee, Minji immediately immersed herself in work. As she read through the onboarding materials, Minji's eyes gravitated towards the company's status report. Without any instruction, she had a strong inclination to read it thoroughly. The more she read, the deeper the frown on her face grew. "This is worse than I thought..."

During lunch, Minji ran into a senior employee in the cafeteria, and their casual conversation led to a shocking revelation. "Come to think of it, you probably don't know, Minji. Mirae Electronics is launching a new smart home system. Our product is now outdated." "Mirae Electronics? Our biggest competitor?" "That's right. And they have a genius strategist named Na Minho. Ever since he joined Mirae Electronics, we've been falling behind."

Minji was deep in thought. On her way home, she searched for news about Mirae Electronics' new product on her phone. The image of Na Minho smiling confidently flashed on the screen. "Na Minho..." she said his name. To

Minji, the name represented a challenge.

It brought back memories from three years ago, when she was 25. At that time, Minji had been running a startup called HomeCozy for about a year. Her goal was to develop an easy-to-use AI-based smart thermostat for households. "Our product is incredibly intuitive. Anyone can use it easily. Every household can enjoy a convenient and energy-efficient life with this" she passionately said to an investor.

"Encouraging individuals to alter their habits is a greater obstacle. How will you overcome that?" an investor said. Around the same time, 32-year-old Na Minho was leading a company called NextFuture and had a competing product. However, his approach was different. Na Minho partnered with large developers and construction companies, supplying his AI-based smart energy management system during the construction of new buildings. He also launched products tailored for commercial facilities and high-rise apartments, mushrooming his market share.

At a startup IR day, Minji watched Na Minho's presentation closely. His strategy was sharp and persuasive, as if he was thinking two or three steps ahead of her. "Our system can reduce energy consumption in large buildings by up to 20%," his confident voice echoed throughout the room. The impressive statement didn't sway Minji, as she remained steadfast in her vision. "So that's another way to consider. We should re-evaluate our methods soon," she resolved.

Yet, reality was harsh. During the final meeting with a major investor, Minji received disappointing news. "CEO Seo, your vision is fantastic. However, we've invested in a B2B model given the current market conditions. NextFuture will be part of our portfolio." Minji couldn't hide her disappointment but lifted her head. "I understand. Thank you for taking the time to review our proposal."

After securing investment, NextFuture grew rapidly and, two years later, was gained by Mirae Electronics. Minji had only heard that Na Minho joined Mirae Electronics as an executive after selling his company. Six months after her failed investment bid, Minji closed HomeCozy. After taking a couple of months to recharge, she joined a global company, where she spent two years gaining new experiences. In her new role, she learned business strategy, market analysis, and the operations of large corporations, which helped her grow in ways she hadn't before.

"Turn obstacles into steppingstones," she often reminded herself. Her experiences strengthened her and became wiser. Finally, Hankook Electronics recognized her skills and recruited her through a headhunter. Now, new challenges awaited her. Competing with Na Minho for investment was a thing of the past, but his name had become a source of motivation, pushing her to surpass her limits.

That night, Minji stayed up late analyzing the company's data. She saw one problem after another with Hankook Electronics. "This won't do. We need a plan."

A few days later, Minji joined a junior board called "Young Innovators," a group recently formed to collect innovative ideas from younger employees and drive change within the company. During her work on the junior board, Minji began investigating Mirae Electronics' new product in more detail. She carefully examined its features, market response, and expert analyses. It was then that she realized the crisis facing Hankook Electronics was more severe than she had initially thought.

"Minji, can you handle this month's executive presentation?" asked Kim, the junior board leader. Minji hesitated for a moment. An executive presentation? Wasn't that too much responsibility? She found herself momentarily speechless. "Are you unsure?" Kim whispered. Minji slowly nodded. "Yes… I'm not sure if I'm qualified for it."

That night, she couldn't sleep. On the one hand, she recognized it as a great opportunity, but fear gripped her. Can I actually handle this important presentation? What if I mess up? Perhaps I should avoid any risks and choose a safer topic instead?" But soon, another voice emerged from within.

"What Hankook Electronics needs right now is change. Someone has to say it. Who else will take the risk and speak the truth if not me?" Minji looked out the window and took a deep breath. She decided. "Alright, let's do it. For Hankook Electronics' future, someone must step up. I can do this." The next morning, she went to see Manager Kim. "Manager Kim, I'll take on the executive presentation." Kim smiled. "Great, Minji. I had faith in you."

As she prepared for the presentation, Minji emphasized the need for change based on her analysis. She stayed up late using strategic frameworks to analyze the current situation and put together a compelling case of why the company needed to change. She also had the desire to examine Hankook Electronics' business portfolio. "Is there a simple way to view the overall business structure?" Then, the BCG matrix popped into her head. She immediately started plotting Hankook Electronics' key businesses on the matrix.

- Stars: Wearable devices
- Cash Cows: Traditional appliances (refrigerators, washing machines, TVs, etc.)
- Question Marks: Smart home systems (in their early stages)
- Dogs: Old feature phone models

After completing her analysis, Minji experienced a sense of shock. Hankook Electronics focused most of its core businesses on the "Cash Cow" or "Dog" categories, leaving a significant gap in businesses that would drive future growth, such as the "Star" and "Question Mark" categories.

"If we continue like this, we're in real danger…" Minji included this analysis in her executive presentation.

On the day of the executive meeting, Minji entered the conference room, visibly nervous. Chairman Kim and the senior executives' sharp eyes were all on her. "I hear the Young Innovators' presentation today was prepared by new manager Minji. What do you have for us?" Chairman Kim issued a declaration. Calming her anxiety, Minji began her presentation. "Yes, Chairman. Based on my analysis, the crisis our company is facing is not a simple temporary downturn. There are structural issues at play." She displayed the strategic framework she had created on the screen.

"Let's first look at the market trends," she pointed to, explaining that this framework comprises four key areas: market trends, customer needs, internal capabilities, and competitor analysis. "The smart home market is growing at an annual rate of over 20%. Meanwhile, our core product line of traditional home appliances is only growing by 2%."

Customer Needs "Second, customer needs," she moved to the next section. Recent surveys reveal that 73% of customers show a preference for integrated smart home solutions. However, our product lineup does not meet this demand."

Internal Capabilities "Third, our internal capabilities," Minji's voice grew stronger. "We have excellent hardware technology, but our software and AI capabilities lag our competitors. If we don't close this gap, we will lose our competitiveness in the future market."

Competitor Analysis "last, competitor analysis," Minji pointed to the last section. "Mirae Electronics' new smart home system is already making waves in the market. Their product is ahead of ours in terms of user convenience, AI features, and energy efficiency."

After a brief pause, she concluded. "In summary, we are in a very dangerous situation. But there's a tremendous opportunity." She paused for a moment before displaying the BCG matrix slide. "I analyzed our company's business portfolio using the BCG matrix." The expressions of the executives grew more serious. "As you can see, most of our core businesses concentrate on the 'Cash Cow' or 'Dog' areas," she pointed out, pausing for a moment before displaying the BCG matrix slide. We severely lack 'Star' businesses to drive future growth or 'Question Marks' with potential." Minji's voice became resolute. "This means our company's future is highly unstable. We need to restructure our business portfolio immediately and find new growth engines."

The room fell into a heavy silence. The executives' expressions became even more somber. In that instant, the head of production spoke. "So, Assistant Manager Seo, in which direction do you think we should go?"

Minji hesitated for a moment before replying, "It's difficult to give a definitive answer right now. But what's clear is that our current strategy won't prepare us for the future. We need to consider entering the smart home market seriously, and we must develop solutions quickly to address our weaknesses.

The marketing director raised concern. "But wouldn't change our core market to be too risky? We could lose our existing customers."

Minji nodded in agreement. "Yes, I understand that concern. But if we don't change, we'll end up losing all our customers. The key is to maintain the strengths of our existing products while expanding into new markets. For example, we could start by adding smart features to our traditional appliances."

Chairman Kim nodded. "Interesting analysis. But isn't there a significant risk in pushing for such a large-scale change?"

At this point, Kang Hyunwoo spoke up. "Chairman, the greater risk lies in not changing. Assistant Manager Seo's analysis is sharp and accurate. If we base a concrete strategy on this, we could achieve significant results."

Chairman Kim looked at Kang. "Coach Kang, what do you suggest we do then?"

Kang smiled and said, "I support Assistant Manager Seo's proposal. I think we should give this young talent a chance. She could help us create a new future strategy for the company."

Finally, Chairman Kim decided. "Alright. Assistant Manager Seo, I'm appointing you as the leader of a new strategic task force. Please work on developing our future strategy. Coach Kang will you mentor Assistant Manager Seo and provide guidance?"

Minji could not hide her surprise as she bowed her head. "Thank you, Chairman. I will do my best."

Kang Hyunwoo also nodded. "Yes, Chairman. I will gladly support Assistant Manager Seo in drawing a new future for Hankook Electronics."

As the meeting ended and people started leaving, Kang approached Minji. "Manager Seo, you were very impressive today. There will be enormous challenges ahead. I'll be here to advise you from outside. Let's overcome this crisis together." Minji nodded. "Thank you, Coach Kang. I have a lot to learn."

"My first piece of advice," Kang continued, "is to start with deeper research on the areas you presented today. Especially customer needs and technology trends. Consider how we can use our strengths in these new markets." Minji nodded seriously. "Yes, I'll get started right away."

As Minji left the conference room, her steps were lighter than ever. She sensed that her true journey was just beginning, and that her real showdown with Na Minho was about to start. As she waited for the elevator, she glanced out the window. The Seoul skyline came into view, with tall buildings that seemed taller and farther away than ever. But instead of fear, her eyes now gleamed with determination.

"Wait for me, Na Minho. I'll beat you and bring Hankook Electronics back to the top." Her eyes shone with resolve. The fierce competition between Hankook Electronics and Mirae Electronics, and the strategic battle between Minji and Na Minho, had just begun. And now, with Kang Hyunwoo as her firm ally, Minji had set out on her journey.

Upon returning to the office, Minji began working immediately. She opened her laptop and began jotting down notes. "1. In-depth analysis of the smart home market 2. Customer needs research – plan focus group interviews 3. Internal capability assessment – recruit software and AI experts 4. Competitor benchmarking – analyze Mirae Electronics' smart home system"

Minji paused for a moment, lost in thought. A hard journey lay ahead, but in her mind, the future of Hankook Electronics was already taking shape. "It's just the beginning," she said. "We will succeed." Her eyes were filled with conviction. The long road to transforming Hankook Electronics' fate had begun.

Explanation of Key Frameworks Used in Chapter 1

3C Analysis Framework

Situations where applicable:
- When considering entry into a new market
- When reassessing existing business strategies
- When responding to changes in the competitive environment
- When planning new products or service development
- When establishing or improving marketing strategies

Purpose

The 3C Analysis Framework is a tool designed to develop effective business strategies by comprehensively analyzing a company's internal capabilities, customers, and competitors. It helps businesses gain a holistic understanding of the market environment and create strategies to secure competitive advantage.

Key Elements

1. Customer
    - Target customer segments
    - Customer needs and desires
    - Buying behavior and patterns

2. Competitor
    - Identifying key competitors
    - Competitors' strengths and weaknesses
    - Competitors' market strategies

3. Company
    - Core competencies and resources
    - Product/service portfolio
    - Company culture and organizational structure

Application Examples:
- When an automobile manufacturer is evaluating entry into the electric vehicle market
- When an online education platform is developing a new learning program
- When a retailer is planning an omnichannel strategy
- When a food company is considering expansion into the health food market

Expected Outcomes
- Enhanced market insights: A comprehensive understanding of the interaction between customers, competitors, and the company
- Development of differentiated strategies: Connecting the company's strengths with customer needs to create effective differentiation strategies
- Risk management: Identifying potential risks in advance by understanding the competitive environment and market trends
- Resource optimization: Focusing on core competencies and enabling efficient resource allocation
- Customer-centric approach: Developing customer-focused strategies through a deep understanding of customer needs

To achieve optimal results with the 3C Analysis Framework, ongoing market research and data collection are indispensable. Also, it's important to analyze from an integrated perspective, considering the interactions between each element. This framework provides more powerful insights when used in conjunction with other strategic tools.

BCG Matrix (Boston Consulting Group Matrix)

Situations where applicable:
- When evaluating and restructuring the company's business portfolio
- When analyzing the strategic position of a product lineup
- When making resource allocation decisions
- When considering entry into new businesses or withdrawal from existing ones
- When planning long-term growth strategies

Purpose

The BCG Matrix is a tool that helps in resource allocation and strategy development by categorizing a company's business units or products based on market growth rates and relative market share. It allows companies to build a balanced business portfolio and promote sustainable growth.

Key Elements
1. Star
- High market growth rate, high relative market share
- Requires significant investment but generates high

returns

2. Cash Cow
   - Low market growth rate, high relative market share
   - Provides stable cash flow with minimal investment and high profitability

3. Question Mark
   - High market growth rate, low relative market share
   - Has growth potential but requires significant investment

4. Dog
   - Low market growth rate, low relative market share
   - Low profitability with uncertain future prospects

Application Examples:
   - When an electronics company evaluates the performance of its diverse product lines
   - When a multinational company analyzes the performance of business units across various countries
   - When an investment firm evaluates the performance

and potential of portfolio companies
- When a food company assesses the market position of its various brands

Expected Outcomes
- Strategic resource allocation: Making appropriate resource allocation decisions based on the position of each business unit or product
- Portfolio balance: Managing a balanced portfolio of businesses at different growth stages
- Identifying future growth drivers: Identifying and nurturing promising 'Question Mark' businesses
- Efficient business restructuring: Making objective decisions about the handling of low-profit 'Dog' businesses
- Optimizing cash flow: Balancing stable income from 'Cash Cows' and investment in 'Stars'

To effectively use the BCG Matrix, regular market analysis and evaluation of the company's position are necessary. Additionally, since the model is simplified, it's recommended to use it with other analysis tools to make more informed decisions.

Episode 2: Surveying with a Bird's-eye View

The newly formed strategy task force office on the 15th floor of Hankook Electronics was buzzing with energy. Minji stood in front of the whiteboard, leading a heated discussion with her team.

"So, based on the data we've gathered, I've completed a PEST analysis," Minji said. "Politically, the recent strengthening of data privacy laws could impact our smart home strategy. Economically, while there are concerns about a global recession, paradoxically, the increased time spent at home is driving up demand for smart home solutions."

Just then, Minji's phone rang loudly. The caller was Park, the manager from the marketing team. "Minji, something big has happened! Mirae Electronics recently announced their AI-based smart home platform, 'MiraeHome AI.' Their stock has already surged by over 15%!" Minji's face stiffened.

Immediately, Minji gathered her task force. "Everyone, the situation has changed. Mirae Electronics has moved faster than we expected. But let's stay calm and continue with our tasks. Let's now re-analyze our position using Porter's Five Forces model."

The team gathered around the whiteboard and began their analysis.

Rivalry among existing competitors: "With the launch of MiraeHome AI, competition has intensified. Our market share is under threat." Threat of new entrants: "Ironically, the strength of Mirae Electronics' product makes it harder for new companies to enter the market." Threat of substitutes: "Traditional home automation systems may quickly become obsolete." Bargaining power of buyers: "Consumers' expectations are rising—they'll demand better services and features, which could be a threat to us." Bargaining power of suppliers: "Key suppliers of AI chips and sensors will probably have stronger negotiation power."

After completing the analysis, the team members looked concerned. A heavy silence filled the room until junior researcher Lee Jooyoung cautiously spoke up.

"But⋯ isn't MiraeHome AI too standardized? That could be a weakness. Not every household has the same needs."

After being lost in thought for a while, Minji slowly brightened. "Jooyoung, that's a brilliant point! Everyone, there might be a breakthrough here. Let's dig deeper into this."

The team began listing the limitations of MiraeHome AI's standardized approach—its failure to account for different household compositions, housing types, and lifestyles, issues with compatibility with existing appliances, and the difficulty of offering personalized services.

Using these insights, Minji proposed a new strategic direction. "What if we focus on a 'customized smart home' strategy? We can offer solutions tailored to the unique needs of each household."

The team's mood lifted. Marketing manager Kim Seojin added, "Yes! With our diverse product lineup, we could offer optimized solutions for each customer."

Armed with this new strategy, Minji presented it to the board, but their reaction was not what she had expected.

"Assistant Manager Seo, your strategy is too defensive," Executive Vice President Kim said sharply. "Mirae Electronics has already captured the market. We need a bolder approach." Minji broke into a cold sweat. "Yes, but our strengths…" "Strengths? Right now, our weaknesses are the bigger problem!" another board member interjected. "How do we expect to compete when we're behind in software and AI technology?" The meeting ended with the board deciding not to adopt Minji's strategy.

Feeling defeated, Minji returned to her office. Right

at that moment, she received a call from Coach Kang Hyunwoo. "Minji, I heard about the meeting today. Don't let yourself get too discouraged. In situations like this, failing fast and learning is crucial. Can we meet at a cafe?" At the cafe, Kang offered Minji a new perspective.

"Minji, your strategic direction is good, but there are a few gaps," Kang said, his tone a mix of warmth and sharpness.

"First, a customized strategy comes with increased costs. How do you plan to maintain profitability? Second, with our lack of AI expertise, how will you deliver personalized services? And finally, have you considered Mirae Electronics' next move? They won't sit still."

For a moment, Minji was speechless when confronted with Kang's incisive queries. But she swiftly regained her composure. "Yes, those are critical points. I hadn't completely taken them into account.

Kang smiled. "Alright then, let's figure out how to solve these issues together. First, how can we reduce the cost of a customized service through modularization?"

The two engaged in an intense discussion late into the night, during which Minji refined her strategy.

Modularized customization: Standardize the base platform but offer additional modules for personalization. AI technology partnership: Propose a strategic alliance with a promising local AI startup. Proactive market segmentation: Target niche markets that Mirae Electronics may overlook.

The next day, Minji stood before the board again with her refined strategy.

"Our goal is a 'modular customized smart home.' We'll standardize the base platform to reduce costs and offer additional modules to provide tailored solutions for each household. As a final recommendation, I propose a strategic partnership with the promising local startup 'DeepHome' to enhance our AI capabilities.

The expressions on the board members' faces brightened. Executive Vice President Kim spoke up, "Excellent, Assistant Manager Seo. This time, your strategy is convincing. Let's move forward with this plan!"

After the meeting, Minji breathed a sigh of relief. She had overcome her first major challenge. Yet she was aware this marked the beginning. The ongoing battle with Mirae Electronics had just begun.

"Watch out, Na Minho. This time, I'll be one step ahead of you."

Minji's eyes burned with determination. The fierce competition between Hankook Electronics and Mirae Electronics had barely started.

Explanation of Key Frameworks Used in Chapter 2

PEST Analysis

Situations where applicable:
- When considering entry into a new market
- When developing long-term strategies for a business
- When assessing the impact of external environmental changes on the company

Purpose
PEST analysis is a tool used to systematically analyze the macro environment of a company. It helps businesses identify external environmental changes and develop strategies to respond effectively.

Key Elements
- Political: Government policies, regulations, political stability, etc.
- Economic: Economic growth rates, inflation, exchange rates, unemployment rates, etc.

- Social: Demographics, lifestyle changes, cultural trends, etc.
- Technological: Technological innovation, R&D activities, automation, technology infrastructure, etc.

Application Example
- When entering the smart home market, considering factors such as the strengthening of privacy laws (P), economic recession (E), increased time spent at home (S), and advancements in AI technology (T).

Expected Outcomes
- A systematic understanding of changes in the macro environment
- Identification of potential risks and opportunities
- Establishment of foundational data for strategy development

Porter's 5 Forces Model

Situations where applicable:
- When considering entry into a new market
- When reassessing the competitive environment of an existing business
- When structural changes in the industry are expected
- When planning long-term business strategies
- When making investment decisions

Purpose
Porter's 5 Forces Model is a framework used to analyze the structure of an industry and assess the intensity of competition within that industry. It helps businesses understand their positioning and develop strategies to secure a competitive advantage.

Key Elements
- Rivalry among Existing Competitors
- Threat of New Entrants
- Threat of Substitutes
- Bargaining Power of Buyers
- Bargaining Power of Suppliers

Application Example
- Analyzing the increase in competition due to a new product launch by Mirae Electronics in the smart home market and evaluating the rising bargaining power of customers.

Expected Outcomes
- Evaluation of industry profitability and attractiveness
- Development of strategies to secure competitive advantage
- Identification of potential threats and preparation of response plans

By effectively utilizing these frameworks, companies can systematically analyze their external environment and industry structure, allowing them to develop effective strategies.

Episode 3: The Omija Princess and the Convenience Store

At 10:30 on a lazy Saturday morning, Lee Jooyoung woke up in her small boarding room in Dongjak-gu. Though she usually led a busy life, she wanted to enjoy a bit of relaxation on weekends. However, by this time, her stomach clock was signaling her to get up. With no particular plans with friends today, she left her hair unwashed, pulled a baseball cap low over her face, and wore comfortable training pants with a white cropped top. As she slid her long, white feet into eco-friendly merino wool sneakers, she trudged out of the house and made her way to the nearby convenience store.

Since joining Hankook Electronics, she hadn't visited the convenience store as often, but on weekends, this place occasionally served as her energy recharge station. Once inside, she picked out a triangle kimbap[1], a cup of ramen, and a banana milk from the shelves. Just as she was about to turn to the register, her eyes glimpsed a brilliantly red omija[2] (fruit of schisandra chinensis, red berries) drink. She stared at it with a blank expression for a while, then finally grabbed a bottle and placed it with her other items on the counter.

After paying, she took a seat at the in-store dining area, poured hot water into her cup of ramen, closed the lid, and gazed out the window, watching passersby. Her eyes then drifted back to the omija drink bottle. It reminded her of her parents, who farmed omija in the countryside, and of her childhood spent there.

The youngest of three children, Jooyoung grew up close to nature. Those experiences deeply shaped her personality and values. Even as a child, she showed a unique perspective on problem-solving. She was particularly obsessed with solving issues related to omija, to where local elders nicknamed her the "Omija Princess."

One day, Jooyoung found her father sighing in the omija fields. "Dad, what's wrong?"

"The birds have eaten all the omija. It looks like this year's harvest will be poor again."

Jooyoung thought for a moment. She discovered old CDs in the shed that evening. "Dad, we can use these to scare away the bad birds!" She tied the CDs with strings and her father hung several of them on the omija trees. The CDs' reflective glare effectively drove the birds away for a while, though the blinding light eventually led older adults to complain, and they had to take them down later.

On another occasion, pests became a problem. Not wanting to use chemical pesticides, Jooyoung recalled a conversation with her grandmother and devised a natural insect repellent with no chemicals. She blended garlic, chili peppers, and vinegar in a mixer to make a spray, which turned out to be surprisingly effective. Limited production made it a temporary solution, but it still served its purpose.

In the fall, during the local festival, Jooyoung created a pamphlet introducing various ways to use omija. "You can make tea, jam, and even use it as a cosmetic ingredient!" Pretending to be on a school field trip, she helped her parents behind the sales booth, confidently explaining the product's benefits. Her confident sales pitch sparked interest and curiosity from many people.

The most talked-about an episode of her childhood that still circulates among people is the high-quality omija dryer she made for a middle school invention contest. Inspired by the drying methods used for herbs and medicinal plants, Jooyoung devised a way to dry omija slowly at low temperatures between 30 and 45°C. Initially, she considered adapting the corn-drying method, but the high-temperature, mass-drying approach used for corn was unsuitable for omija, which needed to keep its nutrients and active ingredients. So, she opted for the herb-drying method instead, which preserved the omija's nutrients and flavor as much as possible, and she even won a prize at the regional science fair. Despite its unsuitability for mass production, this invention remained one of the most meaningful awards she received in her youth, which was enough consolation for her.

Lastly, Jooyoung also proposed ways to use omija by-products. She suggested pressing the seeds for oil and using the peels as compost, promoting a circular use of resources. This made her sense that she was slightly ahead of her time.

These experiences laid the foundation for Jooyoung's problem-solving abilities and creativity.

From the time she graduated high school and moved to Seoul, Jooyoung's life became busy. She enrolled a university in Seoul, majoring in software engineering, with a minor in philosophy to broaden her knowledge of humanities.

University life was never easy. Although she covered tuition with academic scholarships and student loans, she had to work part-time jobs constantly to cover living expenses. From tutoring and convenience store jobs to freelance programming work for small businesses, she did everything she could while also staying dedicated to her studies. She occasionally entered software competitions in her spare time, earning some prize money as a bonus when luck was on her side.

"I'm an adult now, and I don't want to ask my aging parents for money anymore," she often told her friends. "They've already worked hard enough raising three kids. Now it's my turn to contribute and do my part.

Oops. While lost in thought, five minutes had passed since she poured water into the cup noodles. She stirred the slightly soggy noodles, alternating between savoring the ramen and the triangle kimbap, and her mind drifted to a convenience store two blocks away, where she had worked part time for six months before joining Hankook Electronics. In hindsight, her experience there was a pivotal turning point that shaped the person she was today.

A year and a half ago, shortly after she started her part-time job while being a second-year graduate student, Jooyoung began noticing several issues at the convenience store. Wanting to help Mr. Park, the busy yet caring owner who always looked out for the part-timers, she started listing the problems one by one. After two weeks of observation and note-taking, she identified over 20 operational issues. Too many to count. So, she categorized each problem by urgency and importance as high, medium, or low.

"Alright, let's prioritize these problems," Jooyoung muttered to herself.

She singled out the issues that were both urgent and important.

1. Difficulty managing inventory because of a surge of customers during exam periods.
2. Safety concerns from drunken customers causing disturbances.
3. Insufficient stock of lunch boxes and sandwiches during meal times because of high demand.
4. Safety concerns for employees working alone during late-night shifts.
5. Conflicts arising from the sale of age-restricted items like alcohol and cigarettes.

Jooyoung pondered over these five problems. Which problem is most effective to solve? And what am I best suited to tackle?" She deliberated the characteristics and solvability of each issue. Problems like drunken customers or employee safety seemed to require policy changes or external cooperation rather than system-based solutions. The same applied to the issue with age-restricted items.

Inventory management was something she could address using her skills in computer science and data analysis. Plus, solving this issue could tackle both the first and third problems simultaneously.

"Alright, let's focus on solving the inventory management issue," Jooyoung decided. "By analyzing the data and leveraging AI, I can find an effective solution."

Though no one had asked her to, Jooyoung's inventory management system development project began in earnest. The passion and creativity she had shown as a child solving problems in the omija fields came to life once again, like magma that had been bubbling inside her finally bursting forth.

"Mr. Park, may I have a word with you?" Like always, Mr. Park came out to inspect the store's sales and inventory before returning home.

"Sure, what's up?" Mr. Park turned towards the counter where Jooyoung stood, his face a mix of curiosity and puzzlement.

"I've been doing some research, and I think I've found a way to increase our store's revenue and profits," Jooyoung said confidently, enunciating each word clearly.

"Oh, really? What's your idea?" Mr. Park leaned forward, his eyes lighting up with curiosity.

Jooyoung began explaining her plan. Her eyes sparkled like the vibrant red of omija berries, filled with a resolute determination to solve the problem.

"As you know, our main customers are university students, so demand fluctuates a lot. For instance, during exam periods, we see a spike in late-night customers, or during festival times, the demand for lunch boxes and sandwiches surges." Jooyoung paused to gauge Mr. Park's reaction.

"That's right. Sometimes we run out of stock because of that, and other times we lose money trying to clear excess inventory," Mr. Park nodded in agreement, though his expression also seemed to say, "What solution could a young student possibly offer?"

Jooyoung continued, as if expecting Mr. Park's skepticism. "Since I'm studying for a master's in computer science, I can create a demand forecasting program for the food items university students usually buy, if we have the right data. What we need is the last 10 years' worth of food sales data from our convenience store. I'll also need the past 10 years of our university's academic calendar, but I can collect that on my own."

Hearing about data thing made Mr. Park's headache. He had lived his life far removed from anything IT-related. Still, the eager gleam in Jooyoung's eyes intrigued him, despite his uncertainty. "So, you're saying that with past data, you can somehow predict how many kimbaps students will buy in the future?" It was a slow afternoon, with few customers, so Mr. Park grabbed two nearly expired drinks from the fridge, called Jooyoung over to the store's window seat, and sat down beside her.

After taking a sip, Jooyoung continued her explanation, trying to make it as easy as possible for Mr. Park, who wasn't familiar with computers. "If we have the data, we can train an AI system with it." Jooyoung continued her explanation after taking a sip, trying to make it as easy as possible for Mr. Park, who wasn't familiar with computers.

"If we have the data, we can train an AI system with it to make predictions based on academic schedules. This will help us estimate how much of each product we can sell next week or even next month by analyzing past patterns."

Mr. Park remained skeptical, but Jooyoung's enthusiasm had a potent attraction. Additionally, even in the worst-case scenario, the potential loss would be minimal – just a short inventory mismatch. So, he gave her the green light, and Jooyoung's ambitious project officially began.

After several weeks of hard work, Jooyoung completed her AI-based demand forecasting model. The model took various factors into account, such as the academic schedule, weather, and day of the week, and it even generated daily recommended stock levels.

"Mr. Park, now you can use this to check how much stock we'll need for next week," Jooyoung said, presenting her first prediction results.

At first, there were some minor hiccups, but gradually, the results showed. The store experienced fewer lost sales opportunities because of stock-outs, and the losses from overstock and expired items significantly decreased.

Six months later, Jooyoung refined the program, making it so easy to use that even Mr. Park, who was not tech-savvy, could manage it. The program became the secret weapon of his convenience store. Jooyoung's actions for his store deeply filled Mr. Park with gratitude, even though nobody asked her to do it or compensated her.

On her last day, as her planned six-month part-time job ended, Mr. Park expressed his appreciation. "Jooyoung, thanks to you, our store has improved a lot. Consider this a small token of my gratitude." He handed her a white envelope.

Inside the envelope was 1 million won, along with a handwritten note from Mr. Park.

"To Jooyoung, thank you so much for everything during these past six months. The program you designed has revolutionized our store into a highly advanced convenience store, resulting in a substantial increase in our sales and profits. Let me tell you one thing for sure: you're going to become someone important. I'll always be cheering you on–Park Chulsoo."

Jooyoung's eyes welled up with tears. She bowed deeply at a 90-degree angle and brightly exclaimed, "Thank you,

Mr. Park! I'll strive to become a valuable asset to Korea, as you suggested!"

A few months later, Jooyoung was amid hectic job hunting as she neared graduation from her master's program. One day, she received a call from an unknown number. When she answered, a male voice introduced himself as the HR manager of the convenience store franchise's head office. Her workplace was a franchise store, while he represented the corporate headquarters overseeing franchises. The head office had been monitoring franchise stores' sales and profits, and they had noticed that the store where Jooyoung had worked had experienced a sudden increase in sales and profitability. Curious about the secret behind this, a staff member from the head office visited the store and, through conversations with Mr. Park, learned about Jooyoung's contributions. This information has reached the HR team.

It was mid-November, and Jooyoung had just completed her application and interview for a public recruitment position at Hankook Electronics, anxiously awaiting the result. The convenience store headquarters offered her a position in their IT department, where she would take part in the redevelopment of their sales management system.

Jooyoung found herself in a dilemma. Her experience at the convenience store was valuable, and the offer from headquarters was appealing. However, her dream was to use IT technology to solve environmental and energy issues, a passion rooted in her childhood spent playing in nature. Although Hankook Electronics primarily focused on home appliances and telecommunications, they had the foundational technology and a long-standing history that could eventually expand into environmental and energy management.

As Jooyoung pondered her options, a message from Hankook Electronics confirming her job offer finally arrived, clearing away all uncertainty. She began typing a response to the HR manager at the convenience store headquarters.

"Thank you so much for this valuable offer," she wrote, pausing briefly before continuing. "However, I have slightly different goals I want to pursue using IT technology. So, I'm afraid I must decline this opportunity.-Regards, Lee Jooyoung."

Back in the present, Jooyoung finished her omija drink and stared at the empty bottle. The taste of the home it contained mirrored the love for nature and the passion to change the world that still consumed Jooyoung's heart. Yet, she couldn't quite figure out why these memories resurfaced as she handled her late Saturday morning.

She got up, left the store, hesitating briefly. The nice weather compelled her to stay outside. "I can't just stay indoors on a day like this," she decided, and headed toward the nearby riverside park.

Initiating a light jog, Jooyoung took pleasure in the revitalizing air as she ran for around 3 kilometers. Slightly out of breath, she stopped by another convenience store by the riverside and bought a cold energy drink. The area around the store was already bustling with people on picnics and cyclists. She found a parasol to sit under, and as she sipped her drink and took a brief rest in the shade, her phone chimed with a message.

When she opened the screen, it was a message from Minji, her team leader, for the past few months.

"Jooyoung, the weather is so nice today that I came up

to Inwang Mountain[3]. While looking out over Seoul from the top, I suddenly thought of our team, especially you. Reaching out to say hi. Enjoy the day outside and have fun. And thank you for being a part of our team." Along with the message was a gift token for dessert and coffee.

Feeling like she had just won a prize, Jooyoung smiled brightly. It reminded her of the first time she met Minji. "Can I trust and follow a team leader two years older than me?" She had been unsure back then. However, after working with Minji for a few months and experiencing her leadership and passion firsthand, Jooyoung had grown to trust and respect her deeply.

Jooyoung found the biggest and most cheerful emoji in her collection and sent it back with a message. "Thank you, team leader! I'm out jogging right now too, and I'll enjoy the treat!"

Getting to her feet with a radiant smile, Jooyoung began her jog back to her home. The pleasant rest, the reflections on her past, and Minji's heartfelt message had filled her with renewed energy.

Episode 4: Capturing the Customer's Heart

A month had passed since the approval of Hankook Electronics' "Modular Customized Smart Home" strategy. Minji and her team were working diligently to prepare for the implementation of the plan. One morning, shocking news appeared on the screen of Minji, startling her. "Mirae Electronics launches AI voice assistant 'Miraeya'... User satisfaction rate reaches a record high of 98%."

Minji stared at the display in disbelief. Just then, her coach, Mr. Kang Hyunwoo, called. "Minji, you saw the news, right? We have to meet without delay.

At the cafe, Hyunwoo asked Minji a challenging question. "Minji, what is your opinion on our level of understanding of our customers? Do we actually comprehend their wants?"

Minji was momentarily speechless. She had always held the conviction that their strategy was customer-focused, but Hyunwoo's question shook her confidence. "I believed I had knowledge, but upon reflection," Minji cautiously said, "I realize we still have a long way to go."

Hyunwoo agreed. "That's right. While macro strategies are important, we need to listen to our customers' voices at this moment. No matter how urgent things are, we must clear our minds and start again from customer segmentation."

The next day, Minji gathered her team for an emergency meeting. "Everyone, from now on, we will conduct a thorough customer analysis, starting with segmentation." The team began segmenting customers using various criteria. After days of intensive analysis, they identified the following key segments.

1. Tech-savvy millennials living alone
2. Dual-income families with young children
3. Active seniors in pursuit of comfort.
4. Home office professionals
5. Eco-conscious families
6. Security-focused urban residents

Minji created personas for each segment and began drawing a 'customer journey map' that tracked their everyday routines. "Imagine their entire day, from waking up to going to bed. What inconveniences do they experience, and what moments bring them joy?"

The team enthusiastically brainstormed ideas. The whiteboard quickly filled with the day-to-day activities and difficulties of various customers. Minji summarized the primary concerns for each segment.

Tech-savvy millennials living alone:
- Compatibility concerns caused by frequent device upgrades
- Balancing privacy with convenience

Dual-income families with young children:
- Difficulties in remotely overseeing and managing children's safety.
- Obstacles in coordinating complicated schedules and household tasks.

Active seniors in pursuit of comfort:
- Difficulty using complex interfaces
- Need for health monitoring and emergency

response

Home office professionals:

- Blurred boundaries between work and personal life
- Challenges in managing background noise, lighting, and other environmental factors during virtual meetings

Eco-conscious families:

- Difficulty optimizing energy usage
- Complexity in selecting and managing eco-friendly products

Security-focused urban residents:

- Concerns about home security because of frequent absences
- Inconvenience in managing deliveries and visitors

After listing these issues, Minji started a heated discussion with her team. "Which of these problems can we solve best? And which issue, if resolved, would provide the greatest value to our customers?"

Marketing manager Kim Seojin was the first to speak. "In my opinion, the issue of dual-income families is the most urgent. Managing children and schedules is a significant source of stress."

"I agree," UX designer Park Ji-won added.

"But solving this problem requires more than just a technical solution. The key is how to make communication between parents and children more natural."

Researcher Lee Jooyoung chimed in.

"I believe that the home office professionals' issue is important as well." As remote work becomes more accepted, especially for small businesses and startups, this segment is likely to grow significantly."

In the middle of the discussion, coach Kang Hyunwoo entered the meeting room. After listening for a moment, he posed a question. "Good points, but I have a question for you. Which of these issues would be hard for Mirae Electronics' 'Miraeya' to solve?"

Minji took a moment to ponder. Then a brilliant idea struck her. "Exactly! We need to focus on problems that simple voice commands can't solve. For instance, managing children in dual-income families or optimizing the home office environment requires more complex solutions."

Kang Hyunwoo nodded. "You're spot on. Now, let's initiate a concrete analysis of how we can address those problems.

The team dived back into their discussion, eventually arriving at an innovative UX concept: the "Smart Life Orchestrator." This system had the following features:

1. AI-based situational awareness: Real-time tracking of family members' locations, schedules, and health
2. Predictive automation: Using past patterns to proactively execute necessary tasks.
3. Context-based interface: Delivering information in the most appropriate format (voice, text, visual) depending on the situation
4. Cross-device integration: Seamless experience across all devices
5. Privacy safeguards: Allowing users to adjust privacy settings for each feature in a fine-tuned manner.

In response to this concept, the team initiated the development of a prototype. However, they encountered unexpected technical challenges during the process. The AI's accuracy fell short of expectations, and there were severe delays in cross-device integration. Minji felt devastated. "How could this happen? Did we rush things too much?" she wondered.

At that moment, Coach Kang Hyunwoo posed another question. "Minji, failures like this are natural. The key thing is how we overcome them. Revisit the customer's viewpoint once again. What's crucial to them?"

She contemplated, and then a stroke of genius hit her, Minji. "Exactly! What holds significance for customers is not 'technology' but 'trust.'"

Minji immediately took action. Besides refining the technology, she explained the challenges they were addressing to the consumers and involved them in the process of finding solutions. This not only earned the customers' trust but also allowed the team to develop a system with a lower technical complexity, yet one that provided higher customer value.

The 'Smart Life Orchestrator' soared to victory with a resounding success in its launch, capturing the market's enthusiastic response. "Hankook Electronics launches innovative smart home system... Customer satisfaction rate hits 99%."

Watching the news, she let out a deep sigh of relief. Through this experience, she gained a clear understanding of putting the customer first in business strategy. Furthermore, there was more positive news to celebrate.

The company promoted her to manager for her pivotal role in breaking new ground.

Kang Hyunwoo said to her,

"Well done, Minji. But this is just the beginning. Without a doubt, the company Mirae Electronics is preparing for their impending move.

She nodded.

"Yes, I am familiar. We must keep onward."

Her eyes shone with determination as she looked ahead to the upcoming challenge. The fierce competition between Hankook Electronics and the rival company, Mirae Electronics, was entering a new phase.

Explanation of Key Frameworks Used in Chapter 4

Customer Segmentation

Purpose
Customer segmentation is the process of dividing the entire market into smaller groups with similar characteristics. This allows companies to develop products or services that meet the specific needs of each customer group and establish effective marketing strategies.

Key Elements
- Demographic Factors (e.g., age, gender, income)
- Geographic Factors (e.g., location, urban/rural)
- Psychographic Factors (e.g., lifestyle, values)
- Behavioral Factors (e.g., purchasing patterns, brand loyalty)

Situations where applicable
- Setting target customers for new product development

- Planning marketing campaigns
- Designing personalized services for customers
- Developing market entry strategies
-

Application Example
in the Smart Home Market:
- Tech-savvy millennials living alone
- Dual-income couples with young children
- Active seniors seeking comfort
- Home office professionals
- Eco-conscious families
- Security-focused urban residents

Expected Outcomes
- Efficient resource allocation
- Increased customer satisfaction
- Discovery of new market opportunities
- Gaining a competitive advantag

Customer Journey Map

Purpose
A customer journey map is a tool that visualizes the entire process of how a customer becomes aware of, purchases, and uses a product or service. It helps companies understand the full context of customer experience and identify areas for improvement.

Key Elements
- Customer behavior stages (e.g., awareness, consideration, purchase, usage, advocacy)
- Customer thoughts and emotions
- Touchpoints (interaction points with the company)
- Customer pain points and opportunities
- Backstage processes (internal operations supporting the customer experience)

Situations where applicable
- Developing new products or services
- Improving existing customer experiences
- Formulating marketing and sales strategies
- Enhancing customer service quality

Application Example

in a Smart Home User's Day:
- Waking up (AI alarm optimized for best wake-up time)
- Morning routine (automated coffee machine, news briefing)
- Getting ready for work (weather-based outfit suggestions, traffic updates)
- Leaving home (automatic security system activation)
- Returning home (face recognition unlock, optimal indoor environment settings)
- Dinner preparation (recipe suggestions based on fridge contents)
- Bedtime preparation (sleep-friendly environment setup)

Expected Outcomes
- Strengthened customer-centric thinking
- Promoted cross-department collaboration
- Identified service improvement points
- Increased customer satisfaction and loyalty

By effectively utilizing these frameworks, companies can develop and deliver better products and services based on a deep understanding of their customers.

Episode 5: Shimpyo, A New Beginning

The narrow alleyways of Hongdae[4] Entrance[5], beneath an old sign, housed "Maple Cafe," once a local landmark. However, the cafe had recently started losing its vibrancy.

One Tuesday evening, Minji visited the cafe as usual. As she opened the door, the familiar aroma of coffee greeted her, along with a sigh. "Ah, Minji, welcome," said Mrs. Kim Yoona, the owner, her voice tinged with exhaustion. With a worried expression, Minji asked, "Is something wrong?

You've seemed more tired than usual lately."

Yoona hesitated for a moment before answering, "Actually⋯ the cafe is struggling. Fewer customers are coming, and we're being pushed out by the new franchise cafes." She paused and took something out of a drawer—a business card. "A regular customer came by a month ago. After hearing my concerns, he suggested I might be better off closing the cafe."

Yoona handed the business card to Minji. As Minji took it, her eyes widened. It read, "Na Minho, Mirae Electronics."

A month earlier, a long-time regular had visited the cafe. It was Na Minho from Mirae Electronics. Though he had been a frequent visitor during his school days, his busy work life had kept him away recently, so he hadn't crossed paths with Minji, who had become a regular only the previous year. "Oh, it's been a while," Minho greeted with a familiar smile.

Kim Yoona beamed at seeing the long-time customer. "Minho, it's really been a while. I assumed you were too preoccupied to drop by." Minho scanned the area. The lively atmosphere from before was gone, replaced by a somewhat chilly emptiness. "Sorry, I have been around a little. How's the cafe doing these days?" Minho asked cautiously. Yoona sighed. "Don't even get me started. Business has been slow…"

Minho paused briefly before speaking again. "Since it's been a while, may I offer some advice?" Yoona quietly nodded.

"To be honest," Minho continued, "I love this cafe for its charm, and people like me enjoy it. But…" He paused before going on. "It might not match what the younger crowd in Hongdae Entrance is seeking lately." "Really?" Mrs. Kim's expression darkened.

Undeterred, Minho continued, "Big franchise cafes and large bakery cafes are dominating the market with their capital. The cafe scene has become polarized between low-cost chains and high-end specialty cafes, leaving those in the middle, like yours, struggling." Yoona let out a deep sigh. "I see… So what should I do?"

Minho took a deep breath and said, "If I were in your shoes, I'd consider closing the cafe before things get worse. It's not aligned with the customer base in this area anymore, and competition is only going to get tougher. You could try transforming it into something like a brunch or salad bar, but that would mean learning to cook, which isn't easy." Kim's expression grew even darker. Sensing he may have been too blunt, Minho awkwardly pulled out a business card and handed it to her. "If you ever need more advice, call me."

After Minho left, Kim Yoona found herself lost in contemplation. She knew he was right, but it was hard to let go. This cafe was where she had poured her youth and passion. A month later, Minji, another regular, visited the cafe again.

That Na Minho used to be a regular here surprised Minji. But maintaining her composure, she calmly inquired, "So, what plans do you have in mind?" Yoona sighed. "I haven't decided yet. I've put so much of myself into this cafe… I don't want to give up easily." Minji returned the business card, having decided. In contrast to Minho's suggestion, she held the conviction that there was still a way to rescue the cafe. And she decided she would help make that happen.

"Ma'am," Minji began cautiously, "I don't want to overstep, but if you'd allow me, I'd like to help you. I can offer some consulting advice after work, as I have studied a bit of management.

Kim Yoona's eyes widened. "Really? In that case... Can you offer me some advice?"

Minji smiled and nodded. "Of course. Let's figure out a great way to revive this cafe together."

At that moment, Minji sensed a surge of determination. She held the conviction that there was an exceptional value in this cafe that could unlock new possibilities. And through this process, she hoped to grow her own skills as well.

"Shall we get started?" Minji said, pulling out her laptop. "Initially, we must find the problem's root. We're going to use the '5 Whys' technique."

"The 5 Whys?" Yoona tilted her head in confusion.

"Yes, we keep asking 'why' to dig deeper into the issue. You'll see, it's quite interesting. Shall we begin?"

Minji: "Why are regular customers leaving?"

Kim: "Hmm... the new cafes are more appealing, I suppose."

Minji: "Why are they more appealing?"

Kim: "They offer a wider variety of experiences, not just coffee."

Minji: "Why aren't we offering more experiences?"

Kim: "I guess I've been running this place for so long that I've only thought of it as a place to serve wonderful coffee."

Minji: "And why do you think that is?"

Kim: "Well... The other possibilities haven't crossed my mind."

Minji: "Why haven't you explored other possibilities?"

Kim paused for a moment. "I guess I've been stuck in old ways of thinking."

Minji nodded, satisfied. "That's it, Ma'am. The traditional view of what a cafe is has trapped us."

A long sigh escaped Yoona after a brief silence. She appeared to realize something. A soft smile beamed on her face, but it quickly faded. "I see… So, what do we do next?"

Minji smiled confidently. "We need to create a unique value for this cafe. Understanding our customers, the young people in this area, is key. How about we spend the next two weeks researching three things? First, the characteristics and needs of the young people visiting Hongdae Entrance. Also, the artists in this area and their needs. And third, what elements are currently attracting the younger generation?"

Two weeks later, they met again. Yoona and Minji enthusiastically shared their research findings. In summary, they found: "The younger generation is very concerned about the environment. Many are involved in the zero-waste movement. Also, artists say there aren't enough spaces to showcase their work. MZ generation consumers especially care about ethical and eco-friendly brands."

Minji's eyes sparkled. "We've got it! It is my belief that we can establish a fresh identity for the cafe centered on this.

They began brainstorming ideas, centering on the themes of sustainability, art, and community. "We should change the name of the cafe too," Yoona said.

After a brief period of reflection, Minji suggested, "How about we call it 'Shimpyo' (pause)? It could symbolize a place to pause and rest amid a busy life."

"Oh, that's great! So, what exactly will our concept be?"

Minji continued to explain. "During the week, we focus on 'Rest & Eco-Friendly,' and on the weekends, it's 'Connection & Community.' Plus, we'll have ongoing art exhibitions featuring local artists."

Kim's eyes widened. "Wow, that sounds amazing! But... will it really be profitable?"

Minji pondered briefly, then smiled confidently. "Yes, it can be. We'll diversify our revenue streams beyond just coffee." She opened her laptop and began explaining the new revenue model.

1. Core sales: Drinks, bakery items, coffee beans, and in-house eco-friendly goods.
2. Artist collaboration revenue: A 20% commission on artwork sales from the exhibitions.
3. Space rental income: Renting out the space for community events on weekends.
4. Membership revenue: Offering priority access to

lectures, discounts on space rentals, and product discounts.

"This way, we can generate a lot more income than just selling coffee," Minji explained.

Kim felt impressed. "This is amazing, Minji! So, where do we start?"

Minji calmly laid out the plan. "First, we need to reach out to recycling artists and bring in a book club. Then we'll remodel the cafe to fit the 'Rest and Connection' themes."

They immediately set the plan in motion. Minji visited a well-known recycling artist in Hongdae Entrance, "Green Fingers."

"Hello, we'd like to display your work in our new cafe, 'Shimpyo,'" she said.

Green Fingers nodded with interest. "Sounds fun. Can you share further details about the concept?"

As Minji explained the cafe's new vision, Green Fingers' eyes lit up. "That's a fantastic idea. I'd love to exhibit my work there. In fact, I'll even create a special piece just for 'Shimpyo.'"

Meanwhile, Yoona reached out to the local independent bookstore 'Bookmalang' (Book and Soft), successfully securing a book club collaboration.

The remodeling also began. The remodeling also started tearing down walls and exposing the ceiling to reveal the pipes, which gave the cafe a more open and spacious feel. They placed plants throughout and installed movable bamboo partitions, adding a cozy yet sophisticated touch. They set up a small Zen garden in one corner. During the week, they would use the partitions to create private spaces for relaxation, and on weekends, they would use them to separate community activities from the cafe's regular function.

"Wow, it's really transformed!" Minji exclaimed.

Kim Yoona smiled proudly. "Isn't it? It truly seems like a 'Shimpyo' now."

Finally, the opening day arrived. Green Fingers' artwork adorned the walls, and the book club members were engaged in a lively discussion in one corner. Guests loved the zero-waste products on display and for sale in eco-friendly packaging.

"Is this really our cafe?" Yoona asked in disbelief.

Minji smiled. "Yes, it is. This is the new 'Shimpyo' we created together."

Just then, a customer approached them. "I love this place. It's so relaxing, yet there's something really special about it. I saw the membership flyer—how can I sign up?"

Yoona and Minji exchanged bright smiles. They both knew it wasn't just a change, but a whole new beginning.

A few months later, 'Shimpyo' had become a hot spot near Hongdae. Its eco-friendly concept, artist collaborations, and diverse community activities had created a buzz, and revenue steadily increased.

"Minji, I can't thank you enough. Without your help, I never could have imagined such a transformation," Kim Yoona said sincerely.

Minji smiled back. "No, it's thanks to you, too. We achieved this together. It wouldn't have been possible without your courage and willingness to take action."

As Minji left the cafe, her steps seemed weightless. She turned back to look at 'Shimpyo,' glimpsing the vibrant interior through the window. She thought, "Sometimes, minor changes can make a big difference. And that change happens when we all work together."

Thus began the new story of 'Shimpyo,' nestled in a small alley in Hongdae Entrance, offering an authentic place of rest during a busy world. This experience also became a valuable lesson for Minji. Putting theoretical knowledge into practice and collaborating with others to drive transformation not only enhanced her abilities as a consultant but also introduced her to the gratification of assisting others.

'Shimpyo' became more than just a cafe. It was a space where artists could bring their dreams to life, a haven for environmentally conscious people, and a hub for diverse community stories. Above all, it was a literal "Shimpyo," a place where people could pause and rest amidst the hustle and bustle of life.

Explanation of Key Framework Used in Chapter 5

5 Whys Analysis

Situations where applicable
- When identifying the root cause of a problem
- When simplifying complex issues for better understanding
- When aiming to resolve the actual problem, not just its symptoms
- When seeking team consensus on problem-solving approaches
- When using it as part of continuous improvement initiatives

Purpose

The 5 Whys analysis is a systematic technique used to uncover the root cause of a problem. By repeatedly asking "Why?" starting from the surface issue, it allows organizations to dig deeper and identify the fundamental causes, leading to more effective solutions.

Key Elements
- Problem Definition: Clearly define the problem to be analyzed.
- First "Why?": Ask the first "Why?" to understand why the problem occurred.
- Subsequent "Whys?": Continue asking "Why?" based on the previous answer.
- Root Cause Identification: Typically, the team identifies the root cause after five rounds of questioning.
- Solution Exploration: Once the root cause is determined, devise a solution to address it.

Application Example
Problem: Decline in sales at a cafe
- Why did sales decline? → Fewer customers visited.
- Why did fewer customers visit? → They went to a new cafe.
- Why did they go to the new cafe? → The new cafe offers something unique.
- Why does the new cafe offer something unique? → Our cafe failed to innovate.

- Why did we fail to innovate? → We didn't track changing customer needs.

Expected Outcomes
- Identification of the root cause of the problem
- Development of effective and sustainable solutions
- Creation of a shared understanding of the problem among team members
- Enhanced ability to think systematically
- Establishment of long-term measures to prevent recurrence

By using 5 Whys analysis, companies can avoid superficial problem-solving and instead address the underlying causes, leading to more robust and long-lasting improvements. This approach benefits not only short-term issue resolution but also contributes to the continuous growth and improvement of the organization.

Episode 6: Finding the Answers Within

After the successful launch of the Smart Life Orchestrator, Hankook Electronics seemed to regain its vitality. But Minji didn't let her guard down. She knew that Mirae Electronics would soon strike back.

The counterattack came, just as she anticipated. Mirae Electronics began aggressively poaching Hankook Electronics' top talent with irresistible offers.

"Manager, we're in big trouble!" Lee Jooyoung burst into Minji's office, out of breath. "Dr. Kim from R&D and Director Lee from marketing submitted their resignations. They're both joining Mirae Electronics!"

Minji was stunned. Both were crucial to Hankook Electronics—especially Dr. Kim, who had developed the core technology for the Smart Life Orchestrator.

"Jooyoung, contact HR immediately and check the schedule for the next executive meeting."

HR Manager Park Sung-joon arrived at Minji's office shortly after.

"Manager Seo, I've heard. We've been monitoring the situation closely, and we're already working on some countermeasures."

Minji breathed a sigh of relief. "That's good to hear. What are those countermeasures?"

Park nodded and began explaining.

"We're preparing a special retention package for key talent, strengthening career development programs, and reviewing ways to improve work-life balance."

Minji contemplated for a moment. "Steps commendable,

but something seems missing."

Later that evening, Minji sat in a nearby cafe, still preoccupied with the recent departures. As she sipped her coffee, a familiar voice interrupted her thoughts.

"Manager Seo, still here at this hour?"

Minji looked up to see Marketing Manager Kim Seojin standing nearby. She smiled tiredly and nodded.

"Just wrapping up for the day. Care to join me for a bit?"

Seojin agreed and sat down. They sat in silence for a moment, sipping their drinks.

"It seems like things are tense at the company these days," Seojin finally said.

Minji sighed. "Yes, it's been stressful. I just feel like we're missing something important."

After a pause, Seojin confessed.

"To be honest... I've received an offer from Mirae Electronics, too."

Minji looked up in surprise. "You, too? What are you going to do?"

Seojin hesitated. "I haven't decided yet. The offer is tempting, but I still have a strong attachment to Hankook Electronics."

Minji, sensing an opportunity, asked, "What would an ideal work environment look like for you, Seojin?"

"Hmm... A place where I can freely explore my ideas, but also have my personal life respected. A balance between work and life, with opportunities for growth," Seojin said thoughtfully.

Minji nodded, absorbing every word.

"Thank you for being honest with me, Seojin. I'll do my best to see if we can create that kind of environment here."

They exchanged understanding smiles before Seojin left. That conversation sparked a new idea in Minji's mind.

That night, still restless, Minji took a walk by the Han River[6]. As she stared at the water, her phone rang. It was Kang Hyunwoo.

"Minji, sorry to bother you after hours, but I was wondering how things are going lately."

Minji sighed with relief. "It was going fine until recently... but now I'm experiencing a sense of being overwhelmed."

"Oh? I'm nearby. how about I swing by for a quick chat?" Kang offered.

Twenty minutes later, the two sat on a bench by the river, looking out at the water.

"What's been bothering you, Minji? Can you tell me?" Hyunwoo asked in a gentle tone.

Minji said the recent talent exodus, the HR team's plans, and her own frustrations.

Hyunwoo listened closely before posing the question, "Minji, what do you think is the real problem here?"

She paused briefly before providing an answer. "Well, it's Mirae Electronics actively recruiting our key talent."

"That's one perspective," Kang said, reflecting on the matter. "But is there another perspective? Why do you think our employees are accepting these offers?"

She took a momentary break before responding. "It's probably because we're not offering them enough value—not just in terms of salary, but growth opportunities, challenges, or a vision they have faith in."

Kang's eyes lit up. "Precisely. The actual issue isn't external—it's internal. We need to determine the actual value we're providing our employees and whether it aligns with their desires.

Minji's eyes widened in realization. "So, what should we do?"

"First, we need to have a clear understanding of our strengths and weaknesses. Why don't we conduct a SWOT analysis? And to fully grasp how we create value for our employees, we should also carry out a value chain analysis." Kang suggested.

She nodded. "That makes sense. Once we understand where we stand, we can figure out how to offer real value to our employees."

Kang smiled. "Exactly. Remember, Minji, in times of crisis, the answers often lie within. We need to carefully analyze what we already have and determine the best way to make use of it.

The next morning, Minji, filled with renewed energy, called for an immediate team meeting with the HR

Manager Park Sung-joon present.

"Everyone, what we need right now is a clear understanding of ourselves. Let's start with a SWOT analysis to get a precise picture of our current situation and follow that with a value chain analysis to rediscover our core strengths."

Both the team and Park agreed and started working. After several days of intense discussions and analysis, they completed the SWOT analysis.

Strengths:
- 70 years of history and brand trust
- Outstanding hardware technology
- Extensive product lineup
- Stable financial structure

Weaknesses:
- Lack of software and AI capabilities
- Rigid organizational culture

- Slow decision-making processes
- Difficulty attracting young talent

Opportunities:
- Rapidly growing smart home market
- Advances in IoT technology
- The growing demand for eco-friendly products.
- Potential for global expansion

Threats:
- Mirae Electronics' aggressive talent poaching
- Rapidly developing technology trends
- Escalating global competition
- Economic downturn leading to reduced consumer spending

As they discussed the results, Minji had an important realization.

"Everyone, our greatest strength is our people. The 70

years of accumulated expertise and the talent that made it are our core assets."

Park nodded in agreement. "That's right. We've always emphasized this in HR, but I think we've been under-investing in our people lately."

Minji then suggested conducting a value chain analysis. The team divided Hankook Electronics' operations into primary and support activities.

Primary Activities:

- Inbound Logistics: Reliable supply chain management
- Operations: High-quality mass production capability
- Outbound Logistics: Efficient distribution network
- Marketing & Sales: Strong brand power
- Service: Trusted after-sales service

Support Activities:

- Firm Infrastructure: Stable financial structure
- Human Resource Management: Structured training

system
- Technology Development: Continuous R&D investment
- Procurement: Efficient global sourcing

Through this analysis, Minji confirmed that Hankook Electronics' greatest strengths were its "technological development" and "human resource management."

"Our core strengths lie in our technology and our people. We need to invest in and develop these areas further," Minji concluded.

With this insight, Minji proposed developing a "Next-Gen Talent Development Program." The team worked closely with HR to refine the program's details.

Park shared HR's existing plans and how they could synergize with Minji's ideas.

"If we combine your ideas with our plans, we could create a truly powerful program," Park said.

Together, they completed the Next-Gen Talent Development Program, which included:

1. Customized Career Development Plans (Led by HR)
2. Incentives for Innovative Ideas (Led by Minji's team)
3. In-house Venture Program (Co-led by Minji and HR)
4. Flexible Work Environment (Led by HR)
5. Continuous Learning Culture (Co-led by Minji and HR)

Once the program draft was complete, Minji requested an executive meeting two days later to present their proposal.

The next day, during her lunch break, Minji headed to a small park near the office to calm her nerves before the big presentation. As she sat on a bench, Park Sung-joon approached her.

"Manager Seo, fancy meeting you here," he said with a smile.

"Oh, Manager Park. Hello," Minji said.

"How's the presentation coming along for tomorrow?"

"To be honest, I'm nervous. I'm not sure if this proposal can truly differ."

Park thought for a moment before responding. "When I first joined HR, I had similar doubts. Change is always scary and uncertain."

"How did you overcome that fear?" Minji asked.

"By looking into the eyes of our employees—seeing their passion and potential. Think about what your plan will mean to them."

Minji nodded. "That's reassuring. I've been listening to a lot of employees while preparing this plan."

"Then you're on the right track. Understanding and respecting each other—that's what we need to prioritize."

They sat quietly for a while, letting the breeze pass by. Minji felt a renewed sense of determination rise within her.

"Thank you for your advice. I'll convey that in tomorrow's presentation."

The next day, Minji stood in front of the executives. The air in the room was thick with tension, making it hard to breathe. With a deep breath, she started her presentation.

"Executives, over the past few days, our team, in

collaboration with HR, conducted a thorough analysis of our company's current situation. Through a SWOT analysis and value chain analysis, we identified our strengths, weaknesses, and core competencies."

She explained the analysis results and introduced the Next-Gen Talent Development Program. The executives listened attentively, asking questions, which Minji and Park answered with calm precision.

After Minji finished her presentation, there was a brief silence. Then Chairman Kim slowly began clapping.

"Well done, Manager Seo. Your analysis and proposal are both timely and insightful. Let's proceed with implementing this program immediately."

The other executives nodded in agreement.

"Manager Seo, I want you and HR to co-lead this initiative. We'll provide whatever support you need."

Though surprised, Minji nodded resolutely. "Thank you, Chairman. I'll do my best."

With that, Minji and the HR team began the full-scale implementation of the Next-Gen Talent Development Program. Though there were initial challenges, the program soon showed results. Employees who had considered leaving stayed, and even top talent from competitors began knocking on Hankook Electronics' doors.

Three months later, Minji received an urgent call from Chairman Kim.

"Manager Seo, I just wanted to thank you personally. Thanks to your efforts and HR's, we've steered the company through this crisis. I won't forget your role in this."

Overwhelmed, Minji could barely respond. Back at her desk, she received a congratulatory message from Kang Hyunwoo.

"Congratulations, Minji. But remember, this is just the beginning. Mirae Electronics is already planning their next move. We must stay ahead."

Minji nodded to herself; her eyes gleaming with determination. The fierce competition between Hankook Electronics and Mirae Electronics was entering a new phase.

Explanation of Key Framework Used in Chapter 6

SWOT Analysis

Situations where applicable
- When developing a new business plan
- When diagnosing the current state of the organization and seeking improvement
- When conducting a comparative analysis with competitors
- When establishing a market entry strategy
- When driving organizational change or innovation

Purpose
SWOT analysis is a tool used to systematically analyze internal factors (strengths and weaknesses) and external factors (opportunities and threats) to support strategic decision-making. It helps organizations objectively assess their current situation and set future strategic directions.

Key Elements

Strengths
- Internal advantages of the organization
- Superior capabilities or resources compared to competitors

Weaknesses
- Internal disadvantages of the organization
- Areas requiring improvement or lacking resources

Opportunities
- Favorable external factors
- Companies can leverage market trends or changes.

Threats
- Unfavorable external factors
- Elements that pose risks to organizational performance or survival

Application Examples
- A tech startup planning to launch a new product
- A retailer considering entry into the online market
- A university reviewing the potential for creating a new department

- A manufacturer preparing to expand into foreign markets

Expected Outcomes
- Objective assessment: Provides a balanced understanding of the organization's current status
- Strategic direction: Enables the development of strategies that leverage strengths and address weaknesses
- Proactive approach: Facilitates capturing opportunities and mitigating threats
- Decision-making support: Offers clear criteria for making informed decisions in complex situations
- Enhanced communication: Promotes information sharing and consensus among team members

For effective use of SWOT analysis, an honest and objective evaluation is crucial. Additionally, it is important to create and execute specific action plans based on the results. When used in combination with other strategic tools, SWOT analysis can offer deeper insights for organizational growth and decision-making.

Value Chain Analysis

Situations where applicable
- When optimizing the cost structure of a company
- When identifying sources of competitive advantage
- When needing to improve business processes
- When designing new business models
- When considering organizational restructuring

Purpose
Value chain analysis is a tool used to break down and analyze a company's activities to understand the process of value creation and identify the sources of competitive advantage. This allows businesses to assess the efficiency of each activity and enhance overall competitiveness.

Key Elements
Primary Activities
- Inbound Logistics: Procurement and management of raw materials
- Operations: Manufacturing products or creating services
- Outbound Logistics: Storage and distribution of

finished products
- Marketing and Sales: Customer acquisition and sales activities
- Service: Post-sale customer support

Support Activities
- Firm Infrastructure: General management and planning functions
- Human Resource Management: Employee recruitment, training, and compensation
- Technology Development: R&D, product, and process innovation
- Procurement: Purchasing activities for necessary resources

Application Examples
- When an automobile manufacturer aims to improve its production process
- When an IT service company seeks to enhance customer service quality
- When a retail company optimizes supply chain management
- When a consulting firm analyzes its service delivery

processes

Expected Outcomes
- Cost Optimization: Identify cost structures of each activity and improve efficiency
- Discover Differentiation Opportunities: Identify areas where the company can gain an advantage over competitors
- Process Improvement: Detect inefficient activities and develop solutions for improvement
- Support for Strategic Decisions: Provide objective criteria for decisions on outsourcing or integration
- Innovation Facilitation: Explore new ways to create value and enhance competitiveness

To effectively conduct value chain analysis, it is essential to gather and analyze accurate data on each activity. It is also essential for the company to interpret and apply the analysis in alignment with its strategy and industry characteristics. Value chain analysis should be performed continuously and adjusted flexibly in response to changes in the market environment.

Episode 7: Chairman Kim's Mountain Lesson

It was 4 a.m. on an early morning when Chairman Kim glanced at his phone again. He had recently received a message from Chairman Cho of S Trading.

"Sorry, Kim. I've got a family emergency, so today's golf is off. Let's catch up another time."

Kim sighed, wondering how he should spend his

suddenly free Saturday morning. He shut off his alarm and resumed sleeping, later rousing again around 7 a.m. His housekeeper was also on her day off because of the golf outing, so he found himself alone on a leisurely morning.

After stretching, Chairman Kim made himself a simple breakfast—toast with a fried egg and a salad from the fridge. He enjoyed his coffee while sitting on the sofa overlooking the garden, flipping through the newspaper.

He quickly skimmed company reports and read a book, losing track of time until 9:30 a.m. The weather outside was so beautiful that he found it difficult to stay indoors. Then an idea crossed his mind.

"I am considering going for a hike."

He considered going to his usual spot, Cheonggye Mountain[7], but with plenty of time on his hands today, he wanted something more challenging. After checking the map and searching online, he found a longer route that started at Cheonggye Mountain and descended toward Gwanggyo Mountain[8].

"Hmm, this looks interesting. If I start now, I should be able to finish by 5 p.m.," he calculated.

After packing some essentials, Chairman Kim left the house. It was slightly past 10 a.m. when he arrived at the trailhead. The crisp mountain air filled his lungs as he began his ascent. Sunlight streamed through the leaves, casting warm rays on his face. He took a deep breath.

"Looks like I could've been roasting on a golf course instead," he mused with a smile.

About two hours into the hike, Kim encountered his first challenge. The trail split into two, despite the map showing a straightforward path.

"Hmm... This is strange," he mused, evaluating his alternatives.

He hesitated briefly before choosing the correct path. But after ten minutes of steep, rocky terrain, he realized he might have made the wrong choice.

"This isn't right," he muttered, turning back. Upon returning to the junction, he took the left path this time. Soon, the trail became more distinct, and he spotted a sign pointing toward his destination.

"Ha! From a distance, the path seemed straightforward, but up close, it's a winding maze," he chuckled to himself.

At that very moment, his phone rang—it was his secretary.

"Chairman, would you be able to confirm next week's schedule?"

"Ah, sure. Hold on," Kim replied, taking a moment to catch his breath as he checked his phone. There is a crucial meeting scheduled for Monday at 10 a.m.

"Yes, let them know I'll be attending the Monday meeting."

As he resumed hiking, Kim's thoughts wandered to Hankook Electronics.

"Our company is on a fresh path, too. We clearly understand the overall situation, but we will need to decide at each crossroads.

He viewed the ideas of the younger executives at his company as radical, given his experience. Yet Kim prided himself on listening to their voices, even when their proposals challenged long-held traditions.

"I must respect our legacy while embracing change. My role is to guide everyone toward a unified direction," he reflected.

Progressing further along the trail, Kim stumbled upon another fork—this time with three paths. He resisted the urge to follow his gut and approached the signpost instead.

"You always need to check the signs when you're on unfamiliar ground. Merely going in a straight line doesn't guarantee it's the right path."

As he moved on, he reflected on the company's decision-making process.

"We also have to recognize when we're at a crossroads. Knowing we're there is crucial."

By noon, Kim reached a small rest area. He sat on a bench, sipping water and wiping the sweat from his face. Nearby, a middle-aged couple chatted quietly as they sat on another bench. From his backpack, Kim pulled out a cucumber, sliced it in half, and chewed it to replenish his hydration.

"Sir, you must be tired! Here, have some coffee," the husband offered, extending a cup from their thermos.

"Thank you, that's very kind of you," Kim replied with a smile. The sweet aroma of instant coffee tickled his nose. He realized how much better it tasted up in the mountains compared to the expensive specialty coffee he usually drank. For a moment, he forgot about business and simply appreciated the warmth of human connection.

"The world still holds kindness," he pondered.

After a brief break, Kim bid farewell to the couple and resumed his hike. But as time passed, his pace decelerated. Despite maintaining good physical fitness, his late 60s were catching up with him, and his energy waned.

"This is tougher than I anticipated," he admitted to himself.

Then, his phone buzzed with a message from Kang Hyunwoo.

"Chairman, I've prepared a topic for our next coaching session. Let's discuss it then."

Kim sent a reply.

"Got it. I'll ponder over it and come prepared. See you next week."

As he resumed his walk, Kim pondered the situation.

"Even familiar paths require extra preparation when connected to new territory. It's the same with running a company," he mused.

By now, the sun was setting, casting an orange glow over the sky. Kim felt a growing sense of urgency. He found the right path but worried about the diminishing daylight.

"I want to avoid getting lost on a local hike," he reasoned, quickening his pace.

When he finally reached the base of the mountain, passing a spring and a nearby stream, it was well past 6 p.m. Despite the hike not going entirely as planned, Kim had a sense of fulfillment. Standing at the bus stop, he noticed a nearby restaurant serving gukbap[9] (Korean Rice Soup). Indulging in the choice, he entered, found a chair, and contemplated the day's events.

"I might be physically exhausted, but I've acquired a great deal of insight," he reflected as he ordered his meal. While waiting for the food, he pulled out his phone and began typing notes into his memo app.

- Details can wind even on a straight path.
- Opting for a linear route isn't always the correct decision.
- Always check signposts at intersections. More often

than not, the path you're on may not lead to your intended destination.

- When hiking unfamiliar routes, start earlier than necessary and leave time to adjust for unforeseen challenges.
- Compare your location with the map and be ready to make quick decisions.

As the steaming bowl of gukbap arrived, Kim smiled with satisfaction. These lessons reminded him of Hankook Electronics' current situation. He chuckled to himself, wondering if it was only the occupational hazard of being a CEO that made him draw parallels between hiking and business.

"Our company is on a new journey. We've set the broad direction, but we need to remain flexible in the details. We must monitor market conditions and pivot when necessary."

He considered the next steps for the company.

"The company is at a crossroads. To move forward, we need a clear signpost."

Kim pondered over the suitable candidate to lead this

new stage. Minji's face, injecting fresh energy into the organization, came to mind.

"Yes, maybe Manager Seo could handle this. She may lack experience, but her passion is unmatched. I'll have to meet with her soon."

With that decision made, Kim finished the last spoonful of his gukbap, feeling rejuvenated. He pulled out his phone once more and sent a quick message to his secretary.

"Schedule meet Manager Seo Minji for Monday at 11 a.m."

As he left the restaurant, Kim was certain that today's tough hike had been the first step toward a brighter future for Hankook Electronics. Chairman Kim stood up, dragging his weary body. His steps on the way home felt as heavy as water-soaked cotton, but his heart was as light as a feather.

Episode 8: Moving in One Direction

Having gained significant experience, Minji now felt an even greater sense of responsibility. Although Hankook Electronics had overcome a critical challenge with the success of the "Grow Together Talent Development Program," she knew this was just the beginning.

One morning, Chairman Kim called her into his office.

"Manager Seo, what you've achieved is remarkable. But

we still have an enormous challenge ahead. We need to redefine the future direction of our company."

Minji nodded in agreement.

"Yes, Chairman. It's crucial for everyone in the company to align and share a unified direction."

Chairman Kim's eyes lit up.

"Exactly. That's why I'm putting you in charge. I want you to lead the company-wide workshop to establish our new vision and mission. What is your opinion?"

Minji experienced a combination of excitement and introspection. This is a huge opportunity to launch Hankook Electronics into a new era, despite the challenges.

"I'll do my best to prepare for this," she said, determined.

Back at her office, Minji immediately reached out to Coach Kang Hyunwoo.

"Coach, I have the responsibility of leading a company-wide vision and mission workshop. How should I approach it?"

After a pause, Kang responded,

"This is a crucial task, Minji. First, you need to analyze

the company's current state and future trends thoroughly. It's also important to listen to all the stakeholders within the company. Last, using a strategy map to define the vision and mission clearly could help."

In accordance with Kang's advice, Minji started preparing. She assembled a task force composed of representatives from each department. However, she soon encountered unexpected difficulties. Each department had different ideas about the company's future direction, and there were stark generational differences. The gap between long-serving executives and younger employees was noticeable.

Tensions rose during day two of the workshop's discussions on vision and mission.

"We need to focus on strengthening our traditional home appliance market. That's our core strength," argued Production Director Park. "We can't throw away the 70 years of technology and brand value we've built."

"No, we need to explore entirely new markets," countered junior researcher Lee Jooyoung. "We should grow into an AI-driven lifestyle innovation company. The traditional market has become saturated. Without innovation, we won't survive."

Room occupants swiftly split into two camps and fervently debated. Minji struggled with how to bridge the divide.

Then, Marketing Manager Kim Seojin tentatively spoke up.

"Both of you have valid points. We can't abandon our strengths, but we also need to change. How can we combine these two perspectives?"

Minji had a sudden moment of insight.

"Everyone, I think we're missing something. Our strength isn't just in our products. Our true strength lies in the 70 years of know-how, passion, and trust we've built with our customers. If we build on that while embracing new technologies and trends, we can become a company that blends tradition with innovation."

A moment of silence was broken by agreeing voices.

"That's true," Director Park nodded. "Our essence is enriching lives, both then and now."

Lee Jooyoung also agreed,

"Yes, our essence has always been about improving everyday life. Let's discover fresh approaches to accomplish it."

Building on this realization, Minji suggested they create a strategy map.

"Let's take what we've discussed so far and outline our future using a strategy map. We'll define our vision, mission, and specific objectives to achieve them."

As they worked on the strategy map, something remarkable happened. The once-divisive opinions converged. They found a direction that leveraged their existing strengths while exploring new markets. The key theme of "harmony between tradition and innovation" emerged.

That evening, the team came together for a dinner, without alcohol, but the atmosphere remained joyful.

"Hey, Jooyoung! When you stood up to Director Park earlier, weren't your knees shaking?" Seojin joked.

Jooyoung laughed nervously.

"Honestly? My legs were trembling the whole time!"

Director Park laughed heartily,

"I found it refreshing! Witnessing the boldness with which young people express themselves gives me optimism for our company's future.

Minji smiled, nodding along.

"Yes, I think we all learned a lot about each other today. How about a toast with cola to celebrate our teamwork?"

"Oh, look at our boss cracking jokes!" Jooyoung said.

Everyone burst into laughter. Suddenly, Seojin became serious,

"Honestly, I assumed this workshop would be a mere formality. But I've learned so much."

Director Park agreed,

"Same here. At first, I thought it was just another workshop, but I was pleasantly surprised by the deep understanding we shared."

"Exactly," Jooyoung chimed in. "Director Park, your story about developing black-and-white TVs in the '80s was so inspiring. It really showed me how far we've come."

Observing her surroundings, Minji felt a surge of immense pride.

"Everyone, what we've discovered today—this balance between tradition and innovation—this is exactly what makes Hankook Electronics special. Our diversity is our strength."

"Oh, Manager Seo, with the motivational speech!" Seojin clapped in mock applause.

"I should report this to the chairman tomorrow."

Everyone laughed, and Director Park raised his glass.

"Alright, let's toast for real this time. To the future of Hankook Electronics⋯ with cola!"

They all stood, lifting their glasses.

"Hankook Electronics, fighting!"

Laughter filled the room as they celebrated. The differences that once divided them had now united them into a stronger team.

The next morning, Minji arrived at the office early, taking a moment to reflect in the small park near the building. While organizing her thoughts for the last day of the workshop, she spotted Chairman Kim passing by.

"Oh, Manager Seo, you're here early," he remarked.

Minji quickly stood and greeted him.

"Good morning, Chairman."

"Mind if we have a quick chat?" Kim asked, sitting beside her.

"Of course, sir," Minji responded.

Gazing across the park, Chairman Kim started,

"Do you know how our company started?"

Minji replied cautiously,

"Yes, I've read about it, but I'm sure there's more to the story."

Kim smiled and said,

"When my father started this company, his dream was simple: 'To bring convenience to every home.' He saw firsthand how much easier a rice cooker could make a life for stay-at-home parent and was inspired to share that vision."

Minji listened intently, moved by the story. Kim went on,

"When I joined the company fresh out of university, I only did it out of a sense of duty to follow in my father's footsteps. As time passed, I observed the profound impact our products had on people's lives, giving this work true purpose."

He paused before continuing,

"When I took over, we faced a tremendous challenge. With globalization, we had to change. I remembered my father's founding spirit: 'Bring convenience.' That didn't change, but the way we delivered it had to."

Minji nodded deeply. Once again, the theme of "harmony between tradition and innovation" resonated strongly.

Kim turned to her.

"Manager Seo, our roots are strong. However, we must now grow new branches from these roots. Differentiating the constant from the variable is our task."

"Thank you, Chairman," Minji expressed her gratitude and made a promise to ensure that our new vision and mission reflect this spirit.

Kim stood, satisfied.

"I look forward to seeing the results. Now, let's finish the workshop strong."

With renewed determination, Minji rose as well. A new

vision for Hankook Electronics was taking shape in her mind.

The workshop finally ended after three days, giving birth to a new vision and mission.

- Vision: "A company that makes every moment of life extraordinary through technological innovation."
- Mission: "Preserving the values of tradition while continuously innovating to enrich customers' lives."

The strategy map detailed key goals across multiple perspectives:

Financial Perspective
- Build a sustainable growth model balancing stable profits from traditional business with innovative growth.
- Focus on long-term value creation through strategic investments in R&D and infrastructure.
- Allocate resources efficiently between traditional and innovative businesses to create synergy.

Customer Perspective

- Take the lead in creating innovative solutions that meet customers' growing needs.
- Provide more than satisfaction—deliver extraordinary customer experiences.
- Strengthen brand trust by balancing 70 years of tradition with a new, innovative image.
- Maintain open dialogue with customers and integrate feedback into product development.

Internal Processes

- Establish an agile organizational structure to respond swiftly to market changes.
- Accelerate digital transformation across departments to enhance operational efficiency.
- Foster an open innovation ecosystem through partnerships that drive continuous innovation.
- Practice sustainable management by realigning business processes with environmental, social, and

governance (ESG) values.

Learning and Growth

- Nurture creative talent with programs that encourage innovation and bold thinking.
- Enhance diversity and inclusion, creating a culture where different perspectives thrive.
- Foster a culture of self-directed learning with systems that support employees' growth.
- Create knowledge-sharing platforms that promote collaboration across departments and generations.

Through this strategy map, all employees can clearly understand the company's future direction and their role in achieving it. The strategy map embedded the key theme of balancing tradition with innovation across all perspectives, reminding everyone to respect the past while pushing forward into the future.

After the workshop ended, Chairman Kim called Minji into his office.

"Manager Seo, you've done an outstanding job. I didn't expect you to unite everyone so effectively. From tomorrow, we will promote you to the Senior Manager. It's time for you to take on even greater responsibilities for the company."

Surprised and elated, Minji responded humbly.

"Thank you, Chairman. This was a team effort, and I couldn't have done it alone."

That evening, Minji celebrated with her team. As they shared stories and laughter, Minji's phone buzzed with a message from Kang Hyunwoo.

"Congratulations, Minji. Chairman Kim told me the news. But stay sharp—word is that Mirae Electronics will soon unveil their new 10-year vision. We should be ready."

Minji nodded to herself. Her curiosity burned with intensity, eager to uncover Mirae Electronics' next move. As Minji realized that the rivalry between Hankook Electronics and Mirae Electronics was about to enter a whole new level, her sense of competition reignited.

Frameworks Used in Chapter 8

MVC (Mission/Vision/Core Values) Framework

Situations where applicable
- When setting the long-term direction of the company
- When redefining the organization's identity
- When improving or strengthening corporate culture
- When expanding into new business areas
- When motivating employees

Purpose

The MVC framework aims to clearly define the organization's purpose (Mission), future goals (Vision), and guiding principles (Core Values) to provide direction and align the actions of all members. It serves as a foundational tool to guide consistent behavior and strategic decision-making within the organization.

Key Elements
1. Mission

- The organization's reason for existence
- The ultimate purpose the organization strives to achieve
- Expressed in a concise and clear statement

2. Vision
    - The future state the organization aims to achieve
    - Specific, measurable goals
    - Inspiring and challenging enough to motivate members

3. Core Values
    - The principles guiding decision-making and behavior
    - Important beliefs shared among all members
    - Typically expressed in 3-5 key words or phrases

Application Examples
- When a startup is forming its initial organizational culture
- When a large company develops a new business strategy
- When a nonprofit explains its purpose to donors
- When a multinational company formulates its global

strategy

Expected Outcomes
- Organizational Identity: Clearly communicate the organization's purpose and direction to its members
- Decision-Making Criteria: Provide a reference for making important decisions
- Employee Motivation: Inspire participation and commitment by sharing goals and values
- Consistent Operations: Ensure all activities and strategies align with the MVC framework
- Improved External Image: Effectively convey the organization's identity to stakeholders

To effectively use the MVC framework, it requires company-wide participation and consensus. Regularly reviewing and adjusting the framework to reflect changes in the environment is also important. The MVC must be practically implemented in all organizational activities to truly have an impact.

Strategy Map Framework

Definition

A strategy map is a tool that visually represents an organization's strategy, showing the cause-and-effect relationships among strategic objectives aimed at achieving the vision and mission.

Purpose
- Clearly and consistently communicate the organization's strategy
- Visualize the connections between strategic goals
- Help all members understand the strategy and their roles in achieving it

Key Components

A strategy map is generally composed of four perspectives.

- Financial Perspective: Financial goals to maximize shareholder value
- Customer Perspective: Value propositions offered to customers
- Internal Process Perspective: Key processes that

create customer value and improve productivity
- Learning and Growth Perspective: Intangible assets (human capital, information capital, organizational capital) that support change and improvement

How to Use
- Clarify the organization's vision and mission
- Set strategic objectives for each perspective
- Identify and connect cause-and-effect relationships between objectives
- Establish key performance indicators (KPIs)
- Develop execution plans and monitor progress

Expected Outcomes
- Improved Understanding of Strategy: Enhanced understanding through visual representation
- Organizational Alignment: Align the entire organization with the overall strategy
- Efficient Resource Allocation: Ensure resources are allocated according to strategic priorities
- Ease of Performance Measurement: Simplify tracking and managing progress toward goals
- Enhanced Strategy Execution: Improve the

effectiveness of strategy implementation

Considerations for Use
- Develop a customized strategy map tailored to the organization's environment and characteristics
- Regularly review and update the strategy map
- Ensure full participation and understanding from all members

The strategy map is a powerful tool for expressing an organization's strategy clearly and simply, helping all employees understand the direction of the company and their roles within it. It is particularly useful for companies like Hankook Electronics, which aim to balance tradition with innovation, by integrating various goals and achieving organization-wide alignment.

Episode 9: The Crisis of 'Happy Flower Shop'

On a breezy April morning, Kang Hyunwoo stood in front of an old, familiar flower shop near Jamsil Station[10]. The sign, which displayed "Happy Flower Shop", had been there for as long as his recollection allowed. For the past 15 years, every wedding anniversary, he had bought his wife a bouquet from this very shop. But something was different this time. The once lively shop seemed dull and quiet.

As he walked in, a faint scent of flowers greeted him, accompanied by a heavy sigh. Behind the counter, arranging a bouquet, was the shop's owner, Lee Sooyeon. She looked up and smiled faintly.

"Oh, Mr. Kang! It's that time of year again. Time really flies, doesn't it?"

Hyunwoo returned the smile and nodded. "Yes, it does. As usual, I'm here for my wife's anniversary bouquet."

Sooyeon started crafting the bouquet, but concern shadowed her expression.

"How's work? Still keeping busy at your company?"

"Yes, things are steady. But how about you, Mrs. Lee? Your shop seems different, not as lively as before. Is everything okay?" Hyunwoo asked, noticing the shop's decline.

Sooyeon sighed deeply.

"You noticed, huh? Things have been tough lately. Business has been declining for a few years now, and it's getting harder to stay afloat. I'm not sure how much longer we can hold on."

Concerned, Hyunwoo probed further.

"What's been the most challenging part for you?"

Sooyeon's eyes clouded over as she explained.

"It's a lot of things. Online flower delivery services have taken a sizeable chunk of our customers, and young people just don't buy flowers anymore. Furthermore, the economy isn't good, and the rent continues to rise. We're barely scraping by."

Hyunwoo paused, his mind whirring. Despite lacking expertise in floristry, he tapped into his instincts as a business consultant.

"Mrs. Lee, if you don't mind, would you let me help? I'm not a flower expert, but I'd like to explore some ideas with you."

Sooyeon's eyes lit up with hope.

"Really? I'd be so grateful. How can you help?"

Kang smiled warmly.

"First, let's analyze the situation to see where the problems lie. From there, we can brainstorm solutions. I'll prepare some things, and we can meet again in three days.

How does that sound?"

"That would be amazing! Thank you so much, Mr. Kang. I'll be ready whenever you are," Sooyeon replied, grateful for the offer.

Kang left the shop, holding the bouquet for his wife. As the spring breeze carried petals through the air, ideas for saving the Happy Flower Shop bloomed in his mind.

Three Days Later...

Kang returned to the flower shop, carrying his laptop.

"Mrs. Lee, I've done some research, and it looks like the challenges your shop is facing are more complex than I initially thought. Let's look together."

Sooyeon nodded as Hyunwoo pulled up a detailed analysis on his laptop.

Challenges Facing the Flower Shop Industry:

1. Inventory Management Issues

- Short shelf life of flowers leads to losses.
- Difficult to predict demand.

2. Seasonal Demand Fluctuations
   - High demand during holidays (Valentine's Day, Mother's Day, graduations).
   - Low sales during off-peak times.
3. Competition from Online Flower Delivery Services
   - Online services offer convenience and variety.
   - Younger customers prefer online shopping.
4. High Operating Costs
   - Rent, labor, and refrigeration costs add up.
   - Difficult to maintain profitability.
5. Changing Consumer Habits
   - Younger generations favor practical or experiential gifts over flowers.
   - The traditional culture of giving flowers is fading.
6. Flower Price Volatility
   - Prices fluctuate because of weather and supply chain issues.
   - Hard to secure stable profit margins.

7. Lack of Differentiated Services
    - Difficulty offering unique value beyond basic flower arrangements.
8. Weak Digital Marketing Skills
    - Limited presence on social media and online platforms.
    - Hard to attract younger customers.
9. Environmental Concerns
    - The increasing awareness of environmental issues causes some to be hesitant in purchasing flowers.
    - Single-use flowers are wasteful.
10. Economic Uncertainty
    - Luxury purchases, like flowers, decline in tough economic times.
    - Fewer regular customers buying frequently.
    -

Sooyeon looked at Kang, amazed by the thoroughness of his analysis.

"Wow... I hadn't realized just how many layers there were

to our struggles. It's overwhelming."

Hyunwoo nodded.

"Yes, it's a tough situation. But within these problems lie opportunities. We should review them and identify possible solutions."

After taking a sip of tea, he continued.

"Before we jump to solutions, let's start by challenging some assumptions we have about how a flower shop should operate. What if we start over and completely reconsider everything?"

Intrigued and nervous, Sooyeon nodded in agreement.

"That sounds like a good idea. How do we start?"

Hyunwoo wrote "Common Assumptions in the Flower Shop Industry" on the whiteboard.

"Let's list out the things we've always taken for granted about flower shops. I'll start."

He wrote the first point: "Customers take care of the flowers after they buy them."

Sooyeon added,

"How about this one: 'The faster flowers wilt, the more

often customers will return to buy new ones, which helps the shop's sales.'"

They kept brainstorming assumptions:

- Flowers are just decorative (customers don't form emotional connections with them like they do with pets).
- Flower shops can only differentiate themselves by the variety, price, or arrangement of flowers.
- People primarily buy flowers for their appearance or occasion, and their meaning doesn't matter much.
- People only visit flower shops on special occasions.
- Flowers are a luxury item.
- Flower shops operate only as physical stores.
- Only experts can properly care for flowers.
- Flower shops sell flowers—and nothing else.

Once the list was complete, Hyunwoo said,

"Great. Let's question the assumptions and ask, 'Why

not?'. Let's review each one."

They turned their assumptions into new possibilities:
- Why not flower shops offer services to help customers care for their flowers after purchase?
- Why not the longer flowers last, the more customers appreciate the service and come back for more?
- Why not we form emotional connections with customers by treating flowers like pets?
- Why not we differentiate flower shops with unique services beyond price and appearance?
- Why not people sell flowers based on their deeper meanings?
- Why not people visit flower shops regularly, not just on special occasions?
- Why not flower become an essential, everyday item, not just a luxury?
- Why not we sell flowers online or through other channels?
- Why not regular customers care for their flowers like

experts?

- Why not flower shops make more money by offering services beyond just selling flowers?

Kang reflected before continuing,

"Mrs. Lee, how about we take a week to ponder over these new possibilities? We'll return with implementation ideas."

Sooyeon agreed.

"Yes, that sounds like a brilliant plan. I'll ponder these ideas, too.

A Week Later...

They met again and brainstormed solutions based on their "Why not?" questions, coming up with 20 ideas. After narrowing down the most viable ones, they settled on these 10 key concepts:

1. Flower Care Clinic & Membership Service

- Offer regular flower check-ups and care advice for a monthly fee.
- Provide discounts on flower purchases for

members.

- Send seasonal care tips through newsletters.
- B2B service: Regular care and replacement for office, hotel, and restaurant flowers.

2. Flower Language Counseling & Storytelling Service
   - Provide consultations about the meaning and significance of flowers.
   - Attach a mini card explaining the meaning of each flower with every purchase.
   - Create limited edition cards for special seasons.
   - Publish a book on flower meanings for additional revenue.

3. Digital Marketing Enhancement
   - Use Instagram to share daily flower stories and care tips.
   - Create a YouTube series: "Five Minutes with Flowers," featuring seasonal arrangement ideas.
   - Blog posts on caring for flowers, flower meanings, and customer stories.

4. Environmentally Friendly Image
    - Brand the flower care clinic as part of a "Flower Life Extension Program."
    - Hold upcycling workshops using wilted flowers.
    - Switch to biodegradable packaging and promote it.

5. Themed Flower Products
    - Develop unique bouquets for holidays, seasons, and trends.
    - Expand into long-lasting plant products like terrariums and potted plants.

6. Hands-On One-Day Classes
    - Offer flower arrangement and DIY flower box workshops.
    - Generate extra revenue and attract new customers.

7. Local Farm Partnerships
    - Work directly with nearby flower farms for fresh supply.
    - Brand flowers as "local blooms" to differentiate.

8. Corporate & Community Partnerships

- Partner with local companies for regular office flower arrangements.
- Secure large event orders (e.g., weddings, local festivals).

9. Online & Offline Integration

- Launch an online flower ordering and care app.
- Offer "Click & Collect" services, where customers can order online and pick up in-store.

10. Expanded Flower-Related Merchandise

- Sell vases, gardening tools, and home decor items alongside flowers.
- Offer a convenient and comprehensive shopping experience.

Sooyeon looked at Kang Hyunwoo with a surprised expression. "Wow... that's amazing. It brings me great comfort to see that we have developed such a wide range of detailed ideas.

Kang Hyunwoo smiled and replied, "Actually, we need to further refine these ideas to determine if they address structural issues in the flower shop industry and meet customer needs."

Sooyeon nodded. "I believe you're correct. So, which one should we choose?"

Hyunwoo said, "Now, we need to match these ideas with the 10 operational issues we've identified and the 5 recent trends. That way, we can select ideas that not only solve our problems but also meet customer needs." They evaluated each idea by matching it with the flower shop's problems and trends.

Floral Clinic: Solves inventory management issues, offers differentiated services, reflects the trend of growing environmental awareness

Flower Subscription Service: Addresses seasonal demand fluctuations, secures stable revenue, reflects changing consumption patterns of the MZ generation

Online Flower Ordering and Management App: Solves lack of digital marketing skills, secures competitiveness with online flower delivery services

Flower Language Card Service: Provides differentiated services, meets the emotional needs of the younger generation

Plant Care Service: Creates additional revenue streams, reflects the trend of environmental awareness, provides emotional stability

After evaluating all the ideas this way, they selected the top 5 that most effectively solved problems and reflected trends.

1. Floral Clinic
2. Flower Subscription Service
3. Online Flower Ordering and Management App
4. Flower Language Counseling
5. Plant Care Service

Sooyeon said, "To implement these ideas, we might need to change the concept of our shop itself. We might even need a new name."

Hyunwoo suggested with a smile, "How about 'Flora Oasis'? It carries the meaning of rest and healing that flowers and plants provide."

Sooyeon's eyes sparkled. "Wow, that's perfect! It sounds like the ideal name for a fresh start."

Hyunwoo said, "Great. Since it's getting late today, how about we meet again in a few days and plan out enacting these top 5 ideas?"

Three days passed. They met again and worked late, drafting the future of 'Flora Oasis.'

Sooyeon, enthusiastic yet slightly anxious, expressed, "I know what to do, but it still feels overwhelming."

Kang Hyunwoo agreed. "You're right. It might be best to prioritize and implement things step by step. Which one do you want to start with?"

After thinking for a moment, Sooyeon said, "Hmm... The 'Floral Clinic' and 'Flower Language Counseling' seem the most interesting. They perceive the importance of effectively showcasing our expertise."

Hyunwoo nodded. "That's a superb choice. Begin with those two and then gradually introduce the other ideas, too."

Sooyeon's eyes sparkled again. "Yes, I'd like to try that. However... I'm not sure how to start. I'm especially worried about the digital marketing part."

Hyunwoo smiled warmly. "Don't worry. I'll help you. How about starting with something small? Maybe create an Instagram account and post a pretty flower picture every day?"

Sooyeon nodded. "I believe I can manage that. But how should we start with the Floral Clinic?"

Hyunwoo thought for a moment and said, "How about doing a free trial event for your existing customers? A week after they purchase flowers or plants, check in on the condition of their plants and offer care tips. Customers can send you 3-4 photos through the shop's business messenger, and you can provide simple coaching."

Sooyeon's face brightened. "That's a great idea! We can gauge customer reactions and gain experience."

Hyunwoo nodded. "Exactly. And for the Flower Language Counseling, how about starting with simple cards? Include a pretty card with each bouquet that explains the meaning of the flowers and how to care for them."

"Wow, I think customers will love that!"

The two of them sketched out a rough plan for each idea, listing the resources and budget. They also mapped out a step-by-step execution strategy, noting potential challenges and how to address them without going into too much or too little detail.

Closing his laptop, Kang Hyunwoo said, "Good. Let's start with these. We can run these two ideas for two weeks and then meet again to evaluate the results."

Sooyeon happily agreed. "Yes, let's do that. Thank you so much, Mr. Kang."

Two weeks later, Kang Hyunwoo visited the flower shop again. This time, the shop had a slightly distinct atmosphere. The wall displayed a poster with an Instagram hashtag, and the counter had a notice for the "Floral Care Clinic" placed next to it.

Sooyeon greeted Kang Hyunwoo with a bright smile. "Mr. Kang, thank you for coming. You won't believe how much things have changed!"

Hyunwoo asked with interest, "Oh, really? What kind of changes have you seen?"

Sooyeon, excited, responded, "First of all, our Instagram followers increased by 300! I never expected that posting daily flower photos would get such a significant response. And the feedback from customers, including our regulars, who tried out the Floral Care Clinic was amazing. Some individuals are interested in becoming members."

Hyunwoo nodded with a pleased expression. "That's great news! How did the flower language cards do?"

"Oh, they were a big hit, too! Customers kept saying how touched they were by the cards. Few inquired about purchasing the cards separately."

Kang Hyunwoo looked satisfied. "That's fantastic. It's impressive how you've made such a big impact in such a short time."

Sooyeon responded humbly, "It's all thanks to you, Mr. Kang. I am filled with optimism now.

Kang Hyunwoo nodded. "This is just the beginning. As we implement more ideas, there will be even bigger results."

Taking a moment to contemplate, he inquired, "What do

you want to try next?"

Sooyeon thought for a moment before replying, "Hmm... I'd like to try hosting a one-day experience class. People seem to love these kinds of experiences nowadays. And I also want to build an eco-friendly image for the shop."

Hyunwoo nodded with interest. "That's a great idea. One-day classes can attract new customers, and an eco-friendly image aligns perfectly with current trends."

He paused for a moment and then said, "For the one-day class, how about starting with a theme like 'Spring Flower Box Making'? For the eco-friendly image, one possibility is to introduce biodegradable packaging and promote it.

Sooyeon's eyes lit up. "Oh, that's a fantastic idea! When can we start?"

Hyunwoo smiled. "We'll need some preparation time. How about taking two weeks to prepare, and then start the following week? I can help you develop a marketing strategy."

Sooyeon agreed happily. "Yes, that sounds great. I'm really looking forward to it!"

As Kang Hyunwoo stood up, he said, "Alright. Let's

meet again in two weeks to check on the progress. In the meantime, reach out if you have questions."

Sooyeon expressed her gratitude. "Thank you so much, Mr. Kang. Thanks to you, I feel hopeful about the future."

As Kang Hyunwoo left the flower shop, a profound sense of contentment washed over him. He sensed that transforming this small flower shop had the potential to not only result in business success but also infuse fresh energy into the local community. And he experienced a sense of pride for having contributed to that process.

Two weeks later, "Happy Flower Shop" had changed its name to "Flora Oasis" and launched its new services. However, the journey to success was not as smooth as their initial minor victories had suggested.

Despite the official start of the Floral Care Clinic, the customer response was underwhelming and lacking in enthusiasm. Customers were unsure and reluctant to spend additional money on follow-up care for their flower purchases.

The flower subscription service also faced difficulties.

Despite some enthusiastic customers, most were hesitant to subscribe for regular flower deliveries.

The creation of the online ordering app surpassed the initial cost estimate because of unforeseen technical problems, and following its launch, it mishandled orders.

Although the flower language cards were well-received, the production costs exceeded expectations, affecting profitability.

Because of low demand, it was difficult to justify hiring a dedicated staff member for the plant care service.

After a month, Sooyeon sensed a depletion of energy. "Mr. Kang, if things keep going like this, I'm afraid our expenses will far outweigh our revenue. What should we do?"

Kang Hyunwoo, though concerned, responded calmly. "Change always comes with challenges. Our task is to identify causes and find solutions, without giving up."

They sat down together once again to analyze the issues with each service.

As a result of their analysis, they identified several key

improvements:

1. Floral Care Clinic offered free trials, allowing customers to directly experience the value of the service.

2. Flower Subscription Service: They added various price points and subscription frequencies to give customers more options.

3. Online Ordering App: They recruited beta testers to gather real user feedback and made improvements accordingly.

4. Flower Language Counseling: They collaborated with local artists to develop unique and artistic card designs.

5. Plant Care Service: They introduced online consultations and remote care options to enhance efficiency.

They also developed organic ways to connect the different services. For example, flower subscription customers received discounts on the Floral Care Clinic, and the online ordering app made it easier to access the

Flower Language Counseling service. These improvements paid off. After three months, the revenue of "Flora Oasis" rose steadily, and by six months, it surpassed the peak sales of the old "Happy Flower Shop."

The Floral Clinic, now renamed, gained popularity through word of mouth. Highly satisfied customers who could enjoy their flowers and plants for a longer time led to repeat purchases through word of mouth. It was later revealed that customers often felt a sense of guilt or failure when their plants withered, believing they could not care for them. This feeling could either drive them to repurchase or cause them to abandon the shop entirely. This is where the Floral Clinic proved its unique value in retaining and cultivating customers.

Initially, Sooyeon offered the Floral Clinic only to her shop's customers, but as word spread, more and more people—who had purchased plants elsewhere—asked for the service. Eventually, she transformed the service into a membership model, where customers could receive the clinic's benefits for a fee, regardless of where they bought their plants.

The flower subscription service became a stable source of revenue, and the online ordering app gained popularity, especially among younger customers.

One year later, "Flora Oasis" became a local landmark. It wasn't just a place to buy flowers, but a space where people could experience healing through flowers.

Overwhelmed with gratitude, Lee Sooyeon said, "Mr. Kang, thank you so much. You didn't just save the shop—you gave it a new life!"

Kang Hyunwoo smiled and replied, "Your effort was the biggest factor. I just pointed to you in the right direction. Keep innovating and moving forward."

The following year, Hyunwoo visited "Flora Oasis" again for his wedding anniversary. The shop was bustling with lively customers, and Sooyeon greeted him with a bright smile.

"Mr. Kang, welcome! Thanks to you, we're thriving. We're even receiving franchise inquiries now."

Hyunwoo offered his congratulations with a smile and

selected a bouquet. At the checkout, he had a pleasant surprise. The flower language card that came with the bouquet had his name on it.

"Hmm, what's this all about?"

Sooyeon laughed and explained, "It's a special gift for you, Mr. Kang. Thanks to you, we could grow like this. As a token of our gratitude, we created a flower language card named after you. It says 'A flower that symbolizes a strong and wise friend,' reflecting the meaning of your name."

Kang Hyunwoo, deeply moved, couldn't find the words to respond, as he realized that his slight efforts to help a little flower shop had resulted in such a wonderful transformation, filling him with gratitude.

As he left the shop, he thought to himself, "Small changes really can make a big difference. More than anything, I'm glad I'll be able to keep buying my anniversary flowers from the same shop for years to come, even when my wife becomes a sweet old lady."

Holding the bouquet close, he walked through the spring breeze. His steps were lighter than ever, and a new dream bloomed in his heart.

Frameworks Used in Chapter 9

The "Why Not" Approach

Situations where applicable
- When innovative ideas are needed
- When aiming to improve existing business models
- When seeking to discover new market opportunities
- When attempting to break organizational stereotypes
- When creative problem-solving is necessary

Purpose
The "Why Not" approach is a creative problem-solving method aimed at breaking existing stereotypes and generating innovative ideas. By questioning the current state or practices and exploring new possibilities, it enables finding innovative solutions that were previously unconsidered.

Key Elements
- Identifying Assumptions: List common assumptions and beliefs related to the specific field or issue.

- Formulating "Why Not" Questions: Develop "Why Not" questions for each assumption to challenge conventional thinking.
- Evaluating Ideas: Assess the generated ideas in terms of their problem-solving value and feasibility.
- Developing Concrete Solutions: Create detailed action plans for the selected ideas.

Application Example
Innovating the Flower Shop Business Model:
- Assumption: "A flower shop only sells flowers."
- Why Not Question: "Why not offer other products or services alongside flowers?"
- Evaluation of Ideas: Flora Clinic (flower care services) – Expected to enhance customer satisfaction as a unique offering.
- Concrete Solution: Introduce a monthly membership program, create and distribute online flower care education content.

Expected Outcomes
- Discovery of innovative ideas
- Significant improvement of existing business models

- Identification of new market opportunities
- Enhancement of the organization's creative problem-solving capabilities
- Establishment of differentiation strategies for securing a competitive advantage

Through the "Why Not" approach, companies can move beyond traditional thinking, view problems from new perspectives, and find innovative solutions. This contributes significantly to business model innovation, the development of new products or services, and the fostering of an overall culture of innovation within the organization.

Episode 10: The Battle of Innovation

"Alright, everyone. Let's design our 'Smart Life Platform' business model together."

Minji stood in front of a wall filled with business model canvases, pointing to the large space and addressing her team. Their eyes lit up with excitement.

"Let's start with the customer segments. Who are our main customers?" Minji asked.

"Well, it's no longer just the people who buy home appliances," said Marketing Manager Kim. "It's everyone who wants a 'smart life.'"

"Good. Now, what value are we offering these customers?" Minji continued.

"It's more than just products. We're offering comprehensive services that improve their quality of life!" exclaimed Developer Lee. "We're providing smart solutions that cover all aspects of daily living."

Minji nodded as she jotted down the ideas.

"What about our channels? Traditional networks may not suffice.

The brainstorming continued late into the night. They filled in every element of the business model: revenue streams, key resources, activities, and partnerships. A week later, Minji stood before the executives, holding the completed business model canvas.

"Executives, this is the future of Hankook Electronics: the 'Smart Life Platform' business model."

Minji began her passionate presentation.

"We're no longer just a home appliance manufacturer.

We are transforming into a platform company that enhances customers' entire lives."

She explained the core elements of the new business model.

- Platform-based Service: Acting as the central hub that connects all smart devices and services.
- Subscription Model: Offering a comprehensive subscription service that includes both hardware and software.
- Partnership Ecosystem: Collaborating with major content providers to expand service offerings.
- Data-driven Personalization: Using customer data to offer personalized services.
- IoT and AI Integration: Seamlessly controlling all devices and services through AI.

"With this model, we can generate continuous revenue while deeply engaging with customers' lives. By leveraging partnerships, we can speed up innovation and explore new markets."

Smiles spread across the faces of the executives.

"Impressive work, Senior Manager Seo. This model could put us ahead in the market," praised Vice President Kim.

However, Minji's joy was short-lived. The next morning, a news alert flashed on her tablet:

Mirae Electronics unveils a potentially industry-influencing operating system called 'LifeOS.'

Minji's heart sank. Mirae Electronics' newly announced CircleNet system was strikingly similar to her team's Smart Life Platform concept.

"This is... too close to what we've been working on," she muttered.

CircleNet was an AI-based operating system that integrated all aspects of daily life, learning from user habits to optimize services. Its core idea was nearly identical to the Smart Life Platform she had envisioned.

Minji experienced a surge of anxiety. Just then, she received a message from Chairman Kim.

"Senior Manager Seo, at the executive meeting in a month, I'd like you to present how our approach will compete with Mirae's. I trust you."

For the next few days, Minji struggled to find a way forward. Desperate for guidance, she reached out to her coach, Kang Hyunwoo.

"Coach, do you have time? I need your advice," she said, her voice heavy with concern.

"Of course, Minji. What's going on?"

"Mirae Electronics announced a platform almost identical to ours. I'm not sure what to do."

Kang paused for a moment.

"What do you think about their system?"

"Well... it's definitely innovative, but it gives the impression... uniform," Minji replied thoughtfully.

"Uniform? Can you elaborate on that?" Kang pressed.

Minji thought for a moment.

"It seems like they're offering the same service to everyone. But people's needs are so diverse."

Kang's voice grew more animated.

"Exactly! Minji, what are we missing?"

Suddenly, Minji's eyes widened.

"Hyper-personalization...? Tailoring the service to each user's unique needs?"

"Precisely! And what's another potential weakness of their system?"

After some reflection, Minji answered,

"Privacy! Centralizing all their data increases security risks."

Kang chuckled.

"Minji, your ideas are brilliant. Let's shift our focus to 'hyper-personalization' and 'distributed privacy.'"

Minji's face brightened.

"And we let users control their own data!"

"Precisely. Now, how can we turn this idea into a concrete plan?"

Minji thought for a moment.

"What if we use blockchain technology to create a decentralized smart life platform? Personal nodes store the user's data, and AI operates locally, only communicating with the cloud when necessary."

Kang nodded.

"That's an excellent idea. It would improve privacy and stability."

"We could also collaborate with open-source communities to develop customized services," Minji added excitedly.

"Fantastic! That would set us apart from Mirae Electronics. Now, how can we test this idea?"

Minji replied thoughtfully,

"We'll need to run an MVP test. We could launch a prototype to a small user group."

Kang smiled.

"That's a good start. How about involving users in the development process itself? Use an open innovation model."

Minji's eyes sparkled.

"That's a great idea! We'll launch a co-creation project where users help shape the platform."

"Perfect, Minji. Now, let's outline the next steps. How will you execute this?"

They spent the rest of the evening mapping out a detailed plan. Minji felt a renewed sense of energy and confidence.

The next day, she gathered her team.

"We're changing our main selling point to a platform that offers personalized and decentralized smart living."

For two weeks, the team worked tirelessly. They developed an MVP for the project, which they named LifeBlock. They also built an open innovation platform to engage users in the development process. Over the next two weeks, they collected feedback from participants and refined the product.

Late one Friday evening, Minji stood anxiously in the company lobby, waiting for her colleague, Lee Jooyoung.

"Boss, have you been waiting long?" Jooyoung asked, arriving with a flushed face.

Minji's voice carried a hint of uncertainty as she said, "No, I just arrived. But... do you think we'll be okay?" The pressure of presenting LifeBlock to the executives on Monday weighed heavily on her.

"Don't worry, Team Lead. Let's focus on the run for now," Jooyoung replied, flashing a reassuring smile.

The two headed to the Han River Park, where a group of

runners had already gathered. Despite the unfamiliar scene of people in colorful athletic gear stretching and chatting, Minji sensed a feeling of anticipation.

"Is everyone ready? Today's course is up to 12 kilometers. Beginners can aim for 5-7 kilometers, and advanced runners can go for 12. Pace yourselves!" called out the leader.

The group started running. Minji and Jooyoung joined the beginners. As they ran along the riverbank, Minji became immersed in the scenery. The city lights reflecting off the water, the cool breeze, and the rhythmic sound of footsteps all provided a sense of calmness.

While running, Minji's thoughts drifted to the LifeBlock presentation. Minji untangled the ideas and connections in her mind. By the time she had covered 7 kilometers, her legs were tired, but her mind was clear.

As the group wrapped up, Minji and Jooyoung exchanged smiles.

"How was it, Team Lead?" Jooyoung asked.

"Surprisingly good. Running helped clear my head," Minji replied, her face glowing with newfound clarity.

On their way back, Minji realized something important. The project's pressure overwhelmed her. This run had helped her regain her focus and energy.

"Jooyoung, let's come back next week," Minji said with a grin.

"Of course! But let's wait until you've crushed that presentation on Monday first. Then we'll celebrate with another run!" Jooyoung joked.

Minji chuckled. Peace finally found her after weeks.

The Big Day: Executive Meeting

During the executive meeting, Minji confidently addressed the room.

"Board Members, I'm excited to introduce our new vision: the LifeBlock project. It's a completely different approach from Mirae Electronics' CircleNet."

She displayed a comparison chart on the screen.

Feature	Mirae Electron-ics 'CircleNet'	Hankook Electronics 'LifeBlock'
Data Storage	Centralized Servers	Personal User Nodes
Privacy	Centralized Management	User-Controlled Privacy
AI Processing	Cloud-Based	Edge Computing + Optional Cloud
Customization	Limited	Full Hyper-Personalization
Innovation Approach	Closed Development	Open Innova-tion
User Participation	Passive Con-sumers	Active Co-Creators
Scalability	Limited	Infinite Scala-bility
Revenue Model	Subscription	Subscription + App Marketplace + Token Econo-my
Ecosystem	Closed	Open and de-centralized
Security	Centralized Vul-nerabilities	Distributed Se-curity
Service Speed	Network-Dependent	Fast Local Processing

The room buzzed with murmurs of interest. Marketing VP Park spoke up first.

"Senior Manager Seo, CircleNet is already getting major attention in the market. How can we compete?"

Minji responded confidently,

"Our strength is in tailoring experiences to individuals and safeguarding their privacy. While CircleNet offers a one-size-fits-all solution, LifeBlock provides services tailored to each user's unique needs, giving them full control over their data."

Tech Lead Lee raised another concern.

"But won't that reduce performance? Handling everything in local could slow down the system compared to a centralized cloud."

Minji nodded.

"That's why we're using edge computing. Most of the processing happens locally, but the cloud assists when needed. This way, we get fast response times and high performance."

CFO Kim voiced his worry next.

"What about costs? Maintaining a decentralized system like this can be costly."

Minji's eyes lit up.

"Good point. Initial development costs may be high, but over time, we'll save on maintaining centralized servers. Plus, with our token economy, users who contribute to the platform's growth can earn tokens to access premium services."

HR Director Choi chimed in.

"Will users understand and adopt such a complex system?"

Minji smiled.

"Users don't need to understand the technical details. Our intuitive interface and AI assistants will guide them through managing their system easily."

After a brief pause, CEO Park spoke up.

"Senior Manager Seo, what's the market potential for this system?"

Minji took a deep breath before answering.

"That's a critical question. For our MVP test, we used a

unique approach. We created an open innovation platform called the Co-Creation Lab and developed LifeBlock with early adopters."

Marketing VP Park's interest piqued.

"So, you're getting direct feedback from users as you develop the product?"

"Exactly," Minji confirmed. "And the results were remarkable. Ninety-two percent of participants reported that LifeBlock improved their daily lives, and 88 percent rated it as far superior to existing smart home systems."

Nods of approval filled the room. A positive energy spread through the meeting.

"Excellent work, Senior Manager Seo," Chairman Kim said with a smile. "Let's move forward with this project. I want you to lead it."

One month later, Hankook Electronics held a press conference to announce the LifeBlock project. The industry's response was overwhelmingly positive.

Six months after its official release, LifeBlock was a runaway success. The ability to control their data and receive hyper-personalized services thrilled users. The platform gained rapid traction, particularly among privacy-conscious millennials and Gen Z users.

"Hankook Electronics changes the game with 'LifeBlock'... Mirae Electronics scrambles to develop a response product."

Reading the headlines, Minji let out a deep sigh of relief. Yet, she understood that this marked only the start. Innovation's journey continued, with a new challenge ahead.

As she gazed out the window, Minji whispered to herself,

"The real smart life revolution is just starting."

Her eyes glowed with determination, ready for the next phase of innovation.

Frameworks Used in Chapter 10

Business Model Canvas

Situations where applicable
- When developing a new business model
- When reviewing or improving an existing business model
- When creating a business plan for a startup
- When redefining the strategic direction of a company
- When needing a shared understanding of the business model within a team

Purpose

The Business Model Canvas is a visual template that outlines the core elements of a business model. It allows businesses to systematically organize their key components, facilitating the creation of new models or improvements to existing ones. It also enhances communication and idea sharing within teams.

Key Elements
1. Customer Segments: Target customer groups
2. Value Proposition: Core value offered to customers
3. Channels: Ways to reach and deliver products/services to customers
4. Customer Relationships: Types of relationships with customers
5. Revenue Streams: Ways the company generates income
6. Key Resources: Essential resources for business operations
7. Key Activities: Critical actions to execute the business model
8. Key Partnerships: Important collaborations with other entities
9. Cost Structure: Major costs associated with operating the business

Application Examples
- An e-commerce startup designing its new business model
- A manufacturing company transitioning to a service-based model

- An educational institution developing an online learning platform
- A software company considering a subscription-based model
-

Expected Outcomes
- Clear understanding of the overall business model structure
- Promotion of innovative business model development
- Improved understanding among team members of the business model
- Foundation for quick experimentation and pivots
- Effective communication tool for investors or partners

To use the Business Model Canvas effectively, regular updates, team discussions, and validation with market data and customer feedback are essential.

MVP (Minimum Viable Product)

Situations where applicable
- When launching a new product or service
- When testing the market response to an innovative idea
- When entering the market quickly with limited resources
- When aiming to understand customer needs precisely
- When there is high uncertainty about product development direction

Purpose
MVP refers to the initial version of a product with only the essential features needed to deliver the core value. This allows businesses to test customer reactions with minimal resources, validate the development direction, and gather feedback for future iterations.

Key Elements
- Core Features: The minimal set of functions that deliver the core value
- Feedback Collection Mechanism: Methods to collect

user behavior and feedback
- Iterative Improvement Plan: A process for continuously improving the product based on feedback

Application Examples
- Launching a beta version of a mobile app with only essential features
- Conducting a pre-launch survey for a new online service via a landing page
- Testing a hardware prototype with a select group of users
- Running a pilot program for a new educational course

Expected Outcomes
- Reduced development costs and time
- Quick understanding of market response to minimize risk
- Easier verification of product-market fit
- Encouragement of customer-centric product development
- Faster innovation through quick learning and iteration

For successful MVP usage, it's crucial to agree on what constitutes "minimum" and establish a systematic process to quickly collect and act on feedback.

Comparative Analysis

Situations where applicable
- When analyzing competitors' products or services
- When planning a market entry strategy
- When deciding on product improvements
- When benchmarking best practices in the industry
- When considering investment or partnership decisions

Purpose
Comparative analysis is a systematic method for comparing two or more entities based on specific criteria. It helps organizations understand their competitive positioning, analyze strengths and weaknesses, and support strategic decision-making.

Key Elements
- Selection of Comparison Targets: Choosing products, services, or companies to compare
- Criteria for Comparison: Defining comparison factors like performance, price, features, design, etc.
- Data Collection and Analysis: Gathering and organizing

information for each comparison criterion
- Result Interpretation and Strategy Development: Drawing insights from the comparison and using them to inform strategy

Application Examples
- A smartphone manufacturer comparing product features with competitors
- An online retailer benchmarking customer service quality
- A SaaS company analyzing competitors' pricing strategies
- An automotive company comparing fuel efficiency and performance of various models

Expected Outcomes
- Deep understanding of the competitive landscape
- Clear positioning of products or services in the market
- Objective basis for creating differentiation strategies
- Identification of product or service improvement areas
- Insights into market trends and customer preferences

For effective comparative analysis, accurate and objective

data collection is essential, and deeper insights into why differences exist and their significance must be drawn beyond simple comparisons.

Episode 11: The Strategist and the North Star

Na Minho gazed out at the bustling streets of Seoul from his office on the 15th floor of Mirae Electronics' headquarters. The dazzling city lights that had once energized him now reflected the growing turmoil in his heart.

"Seven years... and these last three..." he murmured to himself.

Seven years ago, he had founded FutureNext with nothing but passion. He had worked tirelessly to build the company, securing major investments and attracting industry attention, leading to its acquisition by Mirae Electronics two years ago. It had been a dream exit, one that many would call the perfect game. The joy and relief from achieving that were still fresh in his memory.

But now, standing at another crossroads, Minho found himself torn. Under the terms of the acquisition, he had spent the past two and a half years as an executive at Mirae Electronics, tasked with shaping its future strategy. His sharp instincts, foresight, and decisive execution had turned Mirae into a formidable rival to Hankook Electronics. Yet, despite this success, he couldn't shake a nagging question:

"Am I on the right path?"

After almost three years, the corporate world remained uncomfortable, akin to an unfitting suit. While he occupied an enviable position, the experience was far from comfortable. It wasn't merely nostalgia for the fast-paced, risk-taking startup culture—though he missed the freedom. He couldn't deny that his time at Mirae had helped him grow in ways he hadn't expected.

Minho picked up a glass of whiskey from the table—one of the few times a year he allowed himself a drink.

"So... what's next?" he muttered.

His mind raced with possibilities: Should he extend his executive contract for another two years, as the company proposed? Start a new venture? Shift to full-time investing? Or explore global markets for a new challenge? Perhaps he could even take a break to reflect on what he truly wanted.

Right at that moment, his phone buzzed. A reminder for tomorrow's meeting popped up: preparations for the CES conference.

"Ah, CES..." he murmured again.

The Consumer Electronics Show (CES), held annually in Las Vegas, was the world's largest tech exhibition. This year, Mirae Electronics unveiled an upgraded version of CircleNet, its flagship smart home platform, which was in direct competition with Hankook Electronics' LifeBlock. Both products combined IoT and AI to offer innovative solutions, but each had its own strengths and weaknesses.

Hankook Electronics' swift transformation had always

impressed Minho and was curious about the person behind it. His research revealed that a relatively unknown figure, Seo Minji, was at the helm of the changes. Though she stayed out of the limelight, his network had confirmed that she was the driving force behind the company's innovations.

"Seo Minji..." he repeated, the name rolling off his tongue with intrigue.

A month later, at CES, the energy of the global tech community buzzed through the streets of Las Vegas. Neon signs lit up the hotels, and crowds of businesspeople, startup founders, and tech enthusiasts filled the sidewalks. They engaged in conversations about AI, 5G, and IoT in hotel lobbies, bars, and casinos, while forging partnerships with a firm handshake.

Minho smiled with satisfaction as he toured the Mirae Electronics booth. The new version of CircleNet was attracting plenty of attention, as expected. He walked around and checked out the other booths.

Additionally, at the Hankook Electronics booth, he laid eyes on it—a name badge.

Seo Minji, Senior Manager, Hankook Electronics.

His heart skipped a beat. Finally, he believed the enigmatic figure stood right before him. Minji looked younger than he had expected, with a calm confidence and a warm smile that belied her critical role in Hankook Electronics' recent success.

Minho wasn't wearing a name tag. Minji had only seen him from a distance at an investment announcement event a long time ago or in small photos from news articles, so she did not recognize that the man in front of her was Na Minho.

With his composure intact, Minho introduced himself.

"Hello, I'm Na Minho from Mirae Electronics."

Minji, now aware that her greatest competitor stood before her, remained poised and greeted him warmly. She took a moment to study him discreetly—this was the man whose name had become synonymous with high-stakes tech innovation.

"I've heard a lot about you, Senior Manager Seo. If you have some time during CES, I'd love to discuss industry trends with you," Minho said.

Minji hesitated for a moment before smiling. She knew

this was one of the few spaces where a meeting between competitors wouldn't raise eyebrows. Plus, it offered a rare opportunity to learn more about Minho, who people often described as a towering figure in the industry.

"That sounds good. I was planning to have a simple meal at an Italian restaurant nearby around 5 p.m. How about we meet there?"

Later that evening, at Buddy V's Ristorante in the Grand Canal Shoppes, a Venetian-themed space complete with gondolas, Minho and Minji sat across from each other at a table. There was an initial awkwardness, but the conversation soon picked up.

"I've been quite curious about you," Minho began. "You're often described as the mastermind behind Hankook Electronics' rapid transformation."

His playful tone put Minji at ease. "You appear to be quite knowledgeable," she chuckled. "It's really a team effort."

The conversation smoothly transitioned to the exhibition, followed by discussions on broader industry trends—5G developments, AI applications, self-driving technology, and the rise of 8K televisions. As they discussed the fierce competition between CircleNet and LifeBlock, Minji commented:

Both products excel, and indeed, competition is tough. It's stressful for us, but ultimately, it benefits the consumers, doesn't it?"

Minho nodded in agreement.

"Absolutely. I believe our rivalry is driving the entire industry forward.

Then, an unexpected connection emerged. "By the way, I found out we both share a fondness for the 'Maple Cafe' near Hongdae—now it's called the 'Shimpyo (Pause) Cafe,'" Minho mentioned.

Minji's eyes widened in surprise.

"Really? I spent a lot of time there working on ideas. It's one of my favorite places. How did you know?"

"The cafe owner mentioned it to me last week," Minho replied with a smile. "I used to be a regular there too, although not as often lately. She spoke highly of you, and said your advice saved his business. She was much more enthusiastic about it than the advice I gave her earlier, which was to close shop if things didn't pick up."

Minji chuckled at the notion of the cafe owner gleefully showcasing her intervention, and the lighthearted rivalry between her advice and Minho's. Their shared connection to the cafe melted away the last remnants of formality.

Their conversation became more relaxed as they talked about their personal journeys. Then, Minji brought up something unexpected.

"You know, we almost crossed paths before."

Minho raised an eyebrow.

"Oh? When was that?"

Minji hesitated before explaining.

"A few years ago, I had my startup. We were competing for funding with your company back then."

Minho's memory clicked. He recalled the competition, where his company had secured the investment, leaving the other contender—Minji's startup—behind.

"I'm sorry to learn about that," Minho said sincerely. "We were desperate for funding as well. Honestly, I believe we were simply fortunate. Not solely due to our superiority. It just so happened that we met the criteria the investors were looking for at that time. Even if there is only one winner in a beauty pageant, wouldn't all the other participants still be beautiful in their own ways?"

His humility took aback Minji.

"Wow, that's not what I expected you to say. My impression of you has always been that of a cold, calculating businessperson."

Minho smiled wryly.

"Many people commonly believe that. However, I am simply a human, like anyone else. I make mistakes, have regrets, and sometimes, I get lost, too."

Something sparked Minji's curiosity.

"I see. But you've been incredibly successful at Mirae Electronics."

Minho remained silent for a moment. He hesitated, unsure whether he should share his inner struggles with Minji. However, for some reason, he felt that it was okay to be honest with her at this moment. "Actually, I've been having doubts about my future. The contract I signed with

Mirae is almost up. It's been an enjoyable experience, but sometimes I wonder if this role really suits me."

Minji pondered this. At first, she held the view that it was a trivial issue for someone who had accomplished so much. However, she noticed the sincerity in his eyes.

"You know... I reckon I grasp," she murmured. "It sounds like what people describe as burnout at the peak of success. I've heard it's more common than we think."

Minho nodded.

"Exactly. From the outside, it seems like I've accomplished everything. But something's missing. Unsure of the problem."

Minji reflected on her own journey.

"I get that. In my case, it's distinct—I sense that I'm in the appropriate location. But after dedicating myself for two years, I haven't had the opportunity to deeply reflect on my own needs."

Minho nodded, understanding.

"We've been so focused on running forward that we've forgotten to look within."

They both fell silent for a moment, each lost in their own reflections.

Minji broke the silence gently.

"In my view, everyone has their own path, even though I have less experience than you. Sometimes, if you take the time to pause and reflect, the direction becomes clear. Perhaps you should consider setting aside some time for yourself."

Minho contemplated her words before nodding.

"That's brilliant advice, Minji. Thank you."

The direct mention of her name from him made Minji recoil slightly, but she didn't have any objections. Unusual ease permeated the moment. And Minho, realizing his sudden shift in tone, looked slightly embarrassed too.

Their conversation deepened as they shared experiences and dreams. What had started as a meeting between competitors was now developing into a dialogue between two kindred spirits, both seeking something beyond the material success they had achieved.

Minji asked cautiously,

"Have you thought about your next steps?"

Minho paused, then spoke honestly.

"To be honest, not really. One thing is clear to me. I desire to engage in meaningful actions that have a genuine impact on the world."

Minji smiled understandingly.

"I know what you mean. I had a similar realization before I joined Hankook Electronics."

Minho nodded.

"How did you find your answer?"

Minji thought for a moment.

"I wouldn't say I've found the answer. It's more like... I'm still figuring it out as I go. The important thing is to keep asking the questions and stay open to new possibilities."

Minho's face brightened.

"That's reassuring. It could be that the focus is not on locating the flawless answer, but on consistently exploring and developing.

Time flew by as their conversation grew more intimate. By the end of the evening, they had both gained a deep respect for one another, viewing each other as allies in the same pursuit of purpose, rather than just competitors.

As they stood to leave, Minho extended his hand.

"Senior Manager Seo, this was a great conversation. It seems to me that we are rivals, yes, but also companions on the same path."

Minji smiled warmly as they shook hands.

"I have the same sentiment. I hope we can continue to learn from and inspire each other."

As they went on their separate paths, each returned to their own thoughts, experiencing a sense of lightness, yet engaging in profound introspection.

Later that night, as Minho walked back to his hotel, the frosty January air of Las Vegas brushed against his face. He passed a group of young street performers busking in the chilly weather. Their performance was rough around the edges, but their passion was undeniable. Watching them, Minho realized he couldn't recollect the last instance when he experienced such genuine enthusiasm for something.

As he walked further down the street, he noticed an elderly janitor tidying up the sidewalk. Usually, Minho would have ignored him, but there was something that made him stop.

"Must be tough working out here in this cold," Minho remarked.

The janitor stopped his sweeping and looked up with a warm smile.

"Oh, this isn't tough at all. I enjoy making the streets a little brighter."

It intrigued Minho.

"How long have you been doing this?"

The janitor chuckled.

"I used to be an executive at a big company. After retiring, I desired purposeful endeavors. Now, I clean these streets whenever I can. It's small, but seeing the city clean in the morning makes me feel like I've made a difference."

The man's words deeply moved Minho. As he walked away, he thought about the contrast between the success he had chased and the janitor's humble sense of purpose.

Entering the lobby of his hotel, he noticed a sign for a rare bookstore, Bauman Rare Books. Curiosity piqued, he wandered in. The store had the air of a museum, with the smell of old books and a comforting, quiet atmosphere.

"Welcome," the middle-aged bookstore guide greeted warmly. Minho began browsing. One book caught his eye: a rare, signed edition of Paulo Coelho's The Alchemist. It was a story he had read long ago but had forgotten. Now, holding the book, its message about following one's personal legend resonated with him deeply.

"Oh, that book," the bookseller said, approaching. "It's the book that marked a turning point in my life. It reminded me of the importance of finding the true purpose of life, beyond success or money."

Minho picked up the book and fell into deep thought. He realized that, up until now, he had been chasing success without ever seriously contemplating the true purpose of his life. When he asked for the price, it was over 600,000 won. Although he had intended to just browse before coming in, he found himself paying with his credit card and walking out with the book in hand.

Back in the hotel room, he gazed at the lights of Las Vegas. Amidst the bright, artificial glow, he could make out faint stars in the distant sky. After a long while, he allowed himself to wonder.

"Amidst all these bright lights, have I been missing the genuine star that guided me all along?"

Looking down at the book in his hands, Minho took a deep breath.

"For so long, I've been running on a path someone else drew. But now... it's time to find my compass. Like the janitor, I also aim to make a meaningful impact on the world. Or like those young performers, find the passion that makes my heart race again."

He sat in silence, experiencing a deep sense of clarity wash over him. Tonight, these encounters were not mere coincidences; they guided him toward a new chapter.

"When my three-year term ends, it's time to move on. It's a journey that goes beyond career and delves into self-discovery. It's time to find my true North Star."

Na Minho's eyes gleamed with resolve. Uncharted territories lay ahead, but fear eluded him. He felt the thrill of the unknown stirring in his heart, and he was ready to embrace it.

Episode 12. A Leap into the Unknown

Episode 12: A Leap into the Unknown

With Hankook Electronics' LifeBlock smart home business finally stabilizing in the market, Chairman Kim summoned Minji to his office.

"Senior Manager Seo, thanks to you, our company has taken a great leap forward. But now it's time to think even bigger," he said, his tone firm yet encouraging.

Minji nodded, sensing the gravity of the moment.

"I'm giving you a new mission," Chairman Kim continued. "Find the next major growth driver that will lead Hankook Electronics for the next ten years. The requirement is a market with scarce competition. We need to carve out a unique space for ourselves, a true blue ocean."

Minji paused to consider the challenge.

"Yes, Chairman, but that's easier said than done," she replied, her voice cautious but determined.

Chairman Kim smiled.

"That's why I'm entrusting it to you. If anyone can do it, it's you."

Back at her desk, Minji sat deep in thought.

"Creating new value in an untapped market... How do I even start?"

At that moment, her phone rang. It was Kang Hyunwoo, her trusted coach.

"Minji, how have you been? It's been a while," he greeted her warmly.

"Ah, Coach Kang, perfect timing! I'm actually in the middle of a big dilemma right now," Minji said, proceeding to explain the new mission from Chairman Kim.

After a brief pause, Kang Hyunwoo suggested, "I think there are a couple of tools that could help. Have you heard of the Ansoff Matrix and the CPSE framework?"

"CPSE? That's a new one for me," Minji admitted.

"It stands for Customer, Problem, Solution, Empathy," Kang Hyunwoo explained. "It's a great tool for finding untapped markets by identifying unmet needs that current competitors might be overlooking."

Minji's eyes lit up.

"That sounds like exactly what we need! Can you walk me through it?"

"Absolutely. How about we meet tomorrow and dive into it in more detail?" Hyunwoo offered.

The next day, at a cafe, Hyunwoo drew the Ansoff Matrix and CPSE framework on a whiteboard as he explained them to Minji.

"First, we use the Ansoff Matrix to explore potential market opportunities. Then, we apply CPSE to home in on a specific strategy," he said, his voice steady with confidence.

Minji nodded thoughtfully. "Alright, I'll get the team together and try applying the Ansoff Matrix first."

A few days later, Minji gathered her team.

"Today, we're going to use the Ansoff Matrix to find our next market opportunity," she began, her voice clear as she pointed to the matrix she had drawn on the whiteboard.

She explained the four quadrants of the matrix:

1. Market Penetration: Current products, current markets
2. Market Development: Current products, new markets
3. Product Development: New products, current markets
4. Diversification: New products, new markets

"So, how can we take our current products and technologies and explore new markets?" she asked.

Her team dove into a lively discussion.

"How about expanding into smart factories using our IoT and AI technologies?" one member suggested.

Another chimed in, "The education sector could also be promising. It's possible that we could develop a smart learning platform."

Ideas flowed, and Minji began organizing them within the matrix.

"But" she reminded them, "we're looking for markets where competition is low. Which of these sectors have less presence from major corporations?"

A brief silence followed. Then, a team member hesitantly suggested, "How about healthcare? Specifically, the smart healthcare sector still seems relatively untouched by big players."

Minji's eyes brightened.

"Good point! Smart healthcare is a blue ocean that can leverage our IoT and AI expertise while still being under-explored."

The team began researching the smart healthcare market more thoroughly—its current size, growth potential, and key players.

"This falls into the 'Diversification' quadrant," Minji noted, "but it aligns well with our existing technology, which reduces the risk."

The team agreed, and Minji decided.

"Let's focus on smart healthcare. Now, we'll use the CPSE framework to craft a more detailed strategy."

With the team focused on the smart healthcare sector, they began applying the CPSE framework:

1. Customer: Who are the underserved customers in this market?

2. Problem: What are the specific pain points these customers face?

3. Solution: How can we solve their problems in a way that current solutions don't?

4. Empathy: How can we deeply understand and connect with these customers?

They analyzed existing healthcare services and made a

critical discovery.

"Team lead," one team member said, "most existing healthcare solutions target high-income, highly educated individuals. Blue-collar workers are the ones who need health monitoring the most."

Minji's eyes lit up.

"That's it! We've found a hidden customer segment."

The team dug deeper into the unique challenges faced by blue-collar workers—long working hours, lack of access to clear medical information, and financial constraints were among the biggest issues.

Building on this insight, Minji began outlining a new health management platform called WorkerWell. The platform would feature an intuitive user interface, workplace IoT sensor integration, and AI-powered personalized health advice.

"Let's go with this," Minji declared. "We'll use a B2B2C model, working with companies to provide this service to their employees. That way, we can avoid direct competition with established healthcare providers."

The team's spirit lifted as they sensed the potential

impact of their project.

One month later, on a Saturday morning, Minji, Jooyoung, and Seojin met outside Gyeongbokgung[11] Station for a team hiking trip. They had completed the full conceptualization of the WorkerWell project, and they were now only a month away from presenting it to Chairman Kim.

"Alright, let's take a break from work today and recharge," Minji said cheerfully.

"I'm ready!" Jooyoung said with a smile as she stretched. "How about you, Manager Kim?"

Seojin gave a nervous chuckle. "It's been three years since I last went hiking... so we'll see."

They hiked through Sajik Park[12], passing Hwanghakjeong[13], and headed toward the Tiger Statue[14]. As they climbed, Seojin began to fall behind slightly.

When they reached the statue, they rested, drinking water and wiping sweat from their faces. Inevitably, the conversation turned back to WorkerWell.

"To be honest," Minji admitted, gazing at the Seoul

skyline, "sometimes this project appears to be too much to handle."

Jooyoung nodded. "I have the same sentiment, but I trust you, boss. Thinking about how this project could change lives keeps me motivated."

Seojin, catching his breath, added, "Same here. The challenge and the reward are both real. Moreover, I sense that I am currently the exact target demographic for WorkerWell!"

They all laughed, a light moment that strengthened their bond as a team.

As they continued the climb, Minji asked out of curiosity, "By the way, Jooyoung, what's your dream?"

Jooyoung answered quickly. "I want to leave my mark on the world by contributing to eco-friendly energy solutions using AI. Maybe I will even win a Nobel Prize! Too ambitious?"

"Not at all," Seojin said encouragingly. "As for me... I haven't really thought about my dream outside of work."

Minji smiled warmly.

"Manager Kim, I hope this project helps you discover

what excites you. My dream is to use our technology to make small but meaningful changes in people's lives."

When they reached the final steep section of the climb, Seojin struggled even more, but both Minji and Jooyoung took turns cheering him on.

By 10:30 a.m., they reached the summit, their faces glowing with accomplishment. They paused, soaking in Seoul's view beneath.

"Once WorkerWell is launched, we'll help thousands live healthier," Minji said, gazing at the city.

Jooyoung nodded. "That's what we're aiming for. Just like today- one step at a time, we'll get there."

Seojin added, "Exactly. I couldn't have made it to the top without you two."

As they descended, they discussed the upcoming presentation to Chairman Kim. There were concerns, but the shared trust among them outweighed their fears.

By the time they returned to Gyeongbokgung Station around noon, Minji experienced a renewed sense of energy.

"Today was really refreshing. Together, we conquer any

mountain.

Jooyoung and Seojin grinned. "Agreed! But first, let's get some lunch!"

The three shared a warm laugh, their hearts filled with excitement and optimism for the challenges ahead.

One month later, Minji stood before Chairman Kim, ready to present the WorkerWell project. As she explained the concept and their progress, she noticed the skeptical expressions on some of the executives' faces.

"Interesting idea, Senior Manager Seo," one executive finally said, "but do you think it's realistic?"

Minji met his gaze with quiet confidence.

"Yes. In fact, we've already begun pilot projects with a few small manufacturing companies. The early results are very promising."

Chairman Kim nodded, clearly impressed.

"Good work, Seo Manager. We'll fully support this project. I'd like you to take direct leadership."

Back in her office after the meeting, Minji looked out

the window, taking a deep breath. Another challenge lay ahead, but this time, she didn't feel daunted. She felt excited.

"This is just the beginning," she thought.

"We're going to change the world, one step at a time."

Her eyes gleamed with determination and passion. The journey toward Hankook Electronics' next glorious future had officially begun.

Frameworks Used in Chapter 12

Ansoff Matrix

Situations where applicable
- When developing long-term growth strategies
- When considering entry into new markets
- When expanding or adjusting a product portfolio
- When reviewing risk management strategies
- When making investment decisions

Purpose

The Ansoff Matrix is a strategic planning tool used to identify growth strategies based on the novelty of products and markets. It provides four different strategies for guiding business growth, helping companies explore new market opportunities, set product portfolio strategies, and balance risk and reward.

Key Elements
- Market Penetration: Current products in current

markets
- Increase sales of existing products to current customers.
- Market Development: Current products in new markets
  - Sell existing products in new markets or to new customer segments.
- Product Development: New products in current markets
  - Develop new products for existing markets.
- Diversification: New products in new markets
  - Introduce new products to new markets.

Application Examples
- A smartphone manufacturer considering expansion into emerging markets (Market Development)
- An automotive company expanding its electric vehicle lineup (Product Development)
- An online shopping platform opening physical stores (Diversification)
- A software company encouraging existing customers to switch to a subscription model (Market Penetration)

Expected Outcomes
- Structured approach to growth strategy formulation
- Balanced evaluation of risks and opportunities
- Discovery of new business opportunities
- Support for strategic resource allocation decisions
- Assistance in setting a long-term growth path

To effectively utilize the Ansoff Matrix, companies must carefully assess the risks and potential returns of each strategy, aligning their core competencies and market conditions with the chosen approach.

CPSE Framework

Situations where applicable
- When exploring new market opportunities
- When differentiation is needed in existing markets
- When pursuing customer-driven innovation
- When developing a Blue Ocean Strategy
- When product or service innovation is required

Purpose

The CPSE Framework (Customer, Problem, Solution, Empathy) is an innovative tool designed to uncover non-competitive strategies by focusing on unmet customer needs. It helps identify overlooked market opportunities, develop unique value propositions, and drive customer-centric innovation.

Key Elements
- Customer: Identify customer segments that existing competitors ignore.
- Problem: Discover unresolved problems faced by these customer segments or existing ones.
- Solution: Provide innovative solutions that address

these problems.
- Empathy: Deeply understand and shape customers' perspectives to create meaningful frames.

Application Examples
- A fintech startup developing solutions for underserved customer segments in traditional banking
- An education company building a customized learning platform for students with special needs
- A food company launching products tailored to consumers with specific dietary requirements
- A mobility company designing transport services for individuals with mobility challenges

Expected Outcomes
- Increased likelihood of discovering Blue Ocean markets
- Establishment of a differentiated competitive advantage
- Realization of customer-centric innovations
- Development of sustainable business models
- Simultaneous creation of social and economic value

Successful application of the CPSE framework requires deep customer research and empathy, as well as creative solutions to the identified problems. Continuous validation of ideas and solutions is essential, making this framework highly beneficial for companies that prioritize customer-driven innovation.

Episode 13. Facing the Change Within

Episode 13: Facing the Change Within

Minji stood in front of the mirror, gazing at her reflection. Memories from three years ago, when she first stepped into Hankook Electronics, flooded her mind. The anxious, uncertain expression she once wore transformed into a confident, self-assured one.

"I've genuinely evolved," she reflected inwardly, almost in disbelief.

As she planned her upcoming two-month sabbatical, a well-deserved reward from the company, she reflected on her journey—the pivotal moments where she found solutions in times of crisis, the late nights spent strategizing with her team, and the countless challenges that pushed her to grow.

The day before her departure, Minji met with her coach, Kang Hyunwoo, at their usual cafe.

"Minji, long time no see! How are you? What is the biggest change in you from the past three years?" Hyunwoo asked, his eyes full of curiosity.

Minji paused for a moment. "To be honest, Coach, I surprise myself sometimes. In the past, I used to experience fear when encountering problems, but now... I honestly get excited. I see new challenges as opportunities waiting for me."

Hyunwoo's eyes sparkled. "That's wonderful. What do you believe led to that change?"

"Hmm... I guess it's because I'm no longer afraid of failure. No, it's more than that—I've learned how to learn from failure. Most importantly, I had believers.

Hyunwoo smiled warmly. "I'm glad to hear that. You've tried various strategic tools over the years. Which ones do you believe aided you the most?"

Minji pondered for a moment. "Each tool gave me a new perspective on problems. For example, when I first needed to assess the company's crisis, using PEST analysis and Porter's Five Forces helped me understand the broader industry landscape."

Hyunwoo nodded in agreement. "Yes, that was the starting point for the strategies we developed. What about other moments?"

"When I struggled to understand customer needs, segmentation analysis and customer journey mapping were incredibly useful. That's how we developed the 'Smart Life Orchestrator.'"

"That was a breakthrough," Hyunwoo said with a proud smile. "And after that?"

Minji's eyes brightened. "During the talent retention crisis, SWOT analysis and the value chain model helped us rediscover our strengths and create the 'Grow Together' talent development program."

"Exactly. Sometimes the key is to look inward during times of crisis. Any other moments that stand out?"

"When we were defining the company's vision and mission, the strategy map truly brought everyone together. It was a powerful tool for aligning the entire organization."

Hyunwoo looked impressed. "You've really mastered a range of tools, using them at the right times. What about the WorkerWell project?"

"That's when the Ansoff Matrix and CPSE framework helped us uncover that untapped blue ocean market," Minji said proudly.

"Impressive," Hyunwoo commented. "But using so many tools—wasn't it difficult?"

Minji candidly confessed, "Yes, at times it was challenging to ascertain which tool to utilize in a given situation."

Hyunwoo's eyes gleamed. "That's exactly why I wanted to introduce something new to you today—the Strategy Toolkit Navigator. It's a guideline that helps you choose the right tool for each business situation."

Minji's curiosity piqued. "Really? How does it work?"

"For example, if you're creating a market entry strategy,

Porter's Five Forces or PEST analysis would be ideal. To assess internal capabilities, SWOT or the value chain model works best. And when exploring new markets, the Ansoff Matrix or CPSE framework are perfect," Hyunwoo explained.

Minji nodded thoughtfully. "I see. If I'd had this guide earlier, it might've saved me from a lot of trial and error."

Hyunwoo smiled gently. "But Minji, those mistakes made you the strategist you are today. This navigator is just a guideline. Don't forget the importance of trusting your intuition and experience."

Minji smiled back, filled with gratitude. "I understand. I'll use this navigator on my trip, but I'll also trust my own instincts."

"That sounds like a good plan. What are your hopes for this trip?"

Minji reflected. "Until now, I've focused on solving problems that were handed to me. Currently, I aspire to generate new prospects. I want to experience and sense the pulse of innovation in the U.S. and Europe firsthand. And, of course, I want to analyze situations more systematically using the navigator."

"Great goals. But can I offer you one piece of advice?" Hyunwoo asked.

Minji nodded, listening closely.

"While you're traveling, try to occasionally give your mind a break from focusing on business. Sometimes, inspiration comes from the most unexpected places when you're not actively searching for it."

Minji smiled gratefully. "I'll keep that in mind, Coach. Thank you for all your guidance."

The next morning, at Incheon Airport's departure terminal, Minji walked slowly, pulling her suitcase behind her. A swift glance revealed the last three years unfolding like a film in her mind.

She remembered her nervous first presentation at a strategy meeting, the sleepless nights spent crafting reports, and the triumphant moments shared with her team. Every experience shaped her present self.

She sensed a swelling of emotion in her eyes—gratitude, pride, and a thrilling sense of anticipation for the future engulfed her.

'This is just the beginning. I'll grow into an even better leader, a better person,' she reflected.

Taking a deep breath, she stepped forward, ready to board her flight and embark on a new adventure. Her eyes gleamed with a depth and clarity that hadn't been there before, as she walked toward her next chapter—ready to face whatever challenges and opportunities awaited her in the unknown territories ahead.

Framework Used in Chapter 13

Strategy Toolkit Navigator

Definition
The Strategy Toolkit Navigator is a meta-framework that helps users select and apply the most suitable strategic tools based on specific business situations. It isn't a standalone framework but rather a customizable tool that can be created and adapted for use in various strategic contexts.

Purpose
- To support the selection of the optimal strategy toolkit for different business situations
- To increase the efficiency of business problem-solving processes
- To improve understanding and application of various strategic tools

Key Components
- Situation Classification System: Categorizes business

situations by type.
- Toolkit Database: Details the characteristics and uses of various strategic tools.
- Matching Algorithm: A logic that connects situations to the most appropriate tools.
- Usage Guidelines: Provides instructions for the effective application of each tool.

How to Use
- Understand the current business situation.
- Classify the situation using the situation classification system.
- Check the recommended toolkit via the matching algorithm.
- Review detailed information on the selected toolkit from the database.
- Apply the toolkit following the provided usage guidelines.

Examples of Recommended Toolkits for Different Situations (as used in previous chapters)

Strategy Development

- 3C Analysis (Chapter 1)
- Internal Capability Analysis: SWOT Analysis (Chapter 6)
- Value Creation Process: Value Chain Analysis (Chapter 6)
- Organizational Direction: MVC (Chapter 8)
- Linking Strategic Objectives: Strategy Map (Chapter 8)

New Business Development
- Discover Non-competitive Opportunities: CPSE Framework (Chapter 10)
- Business Model Design: Business Model Canvas (Chapter 10)
- Expansion Strategy: Ansoff Matrix (Chapter 12)

General Situation Analysis
- Macro-environmental Analysis: PEST Analysis (Chapter 2)
- Industry Structure Analysis: Porter's 5 Forces Model (Chapter 2)
- Portfolio Analysis: BCG Matrix (Chapter 1)
- Understanding Customers: Customer Segmentation (Chapter 4), Customer Journey Map (Chapter 4)

Expected Outcomes
- Systematization of problem-solving processes: Helps structure how problems are approached and solved.
- Learning of diverse strategy toolkits: Facilitates the understanding and application of multiple tools.
- Support for optimal decision-making: Provides the right tools for different strategic decisions.
- Strengthening of knowledge sharing and collaboration: Encourages team-based learning and application.

By using the Strategy Toolkit Navigator, business leaders can more effectively address problems and formulate strategies in a variety of situations. This tool not only aids in the selection of appropriate frameworks but also enhances strategic thinking and capability across the organization.

Epilogue

In 2010, when I founded a small management consulting firm, I had various dreams and aspirations, many of which I have pursued and brought to fruition over the past decade. Yet, one aspiration remained unresolved—writing a business novel. It's crystal clear, in my perspective, that the reason for this is straightforward. There is a notable difference between understanding management theories and business concepts as methodologies or tools, and effectively expressing those ideas through storytelling, which is a form of communication that humans are particularly drawn to.

In business and management, much of what we do revolves around understanding problems and finding solutions. However, simply learning concepts in isolation from real-world experience often makes it challenging to apply them effectively when actual situations arise. Of course, with time and accumulated experience, these challenges eventually resolve themselves. Nevertheless, there is a gap.

The classic books that helped solidify my belief in this approach are 'The Goal', a novel embodying the core principles of the Theory of Constraints (TOC), and 'Profit Lessons', a story that vividly illustrates the profit zone framework. Both are examples of business novels—stories written by management scholars, no less. After reading them, one realizes the power of the novel format, not only for its literary value but also for its practical utility in conveying complex ideas.

The companies and characters featured in 'The Queen of Strategy' are entirely fictional. If any readers find themselves reminded of certain proper companies or individuals, I would like to clarify in advance that such resemblances are purely coincidental. The novel is not based on any specific entity or person.

Despite being a fictional story, the strategic decision-making and innovation processes depicted in the narrative are not without meaning. Readers will find themselves engrossed in the tale, empathizing with Minji as she navigates the complexities of leadership and drives an established company toward the future. In doing so, I hope readers will discover their own insights and learnings.

In this business novel, I focused on fully developing the characters. In addition, I have included separate chapters to explain the various management tools featured in the story, enhancing utilising the content. For instance, in Chapter 9, I introduced the problem-solving approach based on "Why Not" questioning, and in Chapter 12, the non-competitive strategy framework based on CPSE. Both methods are ones I have developed and use in my consulting practice. For those curious about these and other approaches, visit The Innovation Lab's website (https://thelab.center).

I sincerely hope that you enjoyed this novel, which follows Minji, a member of the MZ generation, as she faces challenges and grows as a strategist.

- Yours sincerely,

Cho Yongho

Acknowledgements

Foremost, I am deeply grateful to my beloved family.

I also extend my heartfelt thanks to all those who have shared and contributed to my experiences in innovation over the past decade, and to everyone who has inspired this book.

The Innovation Lab®: Our Work

At The Innovation Lab, we believe that through the processes of viewing, thinking, acting, and creating differently, we can achieve meaningful change.

Since our inception in 2010, The Innovation Lab has been systematically integrating innovative mindsets, techniques, tools, and methodologies to bridge the latest management theories with real-world business performance.

- Website   https://thelab.center
- Email   brad.cho@visionarena.co.kr

How to Use the Queen of Strategy GPTs

We have created an AI-based chatbot that allows you to engage in a simulated conversation with Minji, the protagonist of The Queen of Strategy. You can access the chatbot for free by scanning the QR code below. After entering some basic information, you'll be able to experience an interactive dialogue with Minji. Enjoy your conversation!

Footnote

1 Kimbap: A popular Korean dish consisting of cooked rice and various ingredients (vegetables, egg, meat, or fish) rolled in dried seaweed sheets (gim) and sliced into bite-sized pieces. While similar in appearance to Japanese sushi rolls, gimbap uses sesame oil-seasoned rice and typically includes cooked ingredients rather than raw fish. It's a beloved convenience food in Korea, commonly enjoyed as a quick meal, picnic food, or snack, available in numerous varieties such as traditional, vegetable, tuna, or cheese gimbap.

2 Omija: A traditional Korean berry with five distinct flavors (sweet, sour, salty, bitter, and pungent). Its scientific name is Schisandra chinensis. The name literally means "five-flavor berry" in Korean. It's commonly used in traditional medicine and as a tea ingredient.

3 Inwangsan: A 338-meter granite mountain located in central Seoul, South Korea. Historically significant as one of the "Four Inner Mountains" that surrounded the old Seoul city wall during the Joseon Dynasty. Known for its distinctive rock formations and traditional Feng Shui (harmony through spatial arrangement) importance in Seoul's geography.

4 Hongdae: An abbreviation of 'Hongik University', a prominent private university located in Seoul, South Korea, known for its strong emphasis on fine arts and design. The institution is widely regarded for fostering creative and practical skills among its students. It also contributes significantly to various academic fields, including engineering and business.

5 Hongdae Entrance: The area surrounding Hongik University's main entrance, known as one of Seoul's most vibrant entertainment and cultural districts. Famous for its indie music scene, street performances, artistic atmosphere, trendy shops, and bustling nightlife. Popular among young people and tourists.

6 Han River: The major river flowing through Seoul, South Korea. It's 514 km long and has played a crucial role in Korean history, commerce, and culture. The river divides Seoul into north and south, and its banks feature numerous parks, recreational facilities, and cultural spaces. It was central to South Korea's economic development, often called the

"Miracle on the Han River".

7 Cheonggyesan: A 618-meter mountain located in Gyeonggi Province, spanning across Seongnam and Seoul. Popular for hiking trails and appreciated as a "green lung" for the metropolitan area. The name means "Clear Valley Mountain" and it's particularly favored by urban residents for its accessibility and well-maintained trails.

8 Gwanggyosan: A 582-meter mountain located in Suwon and Yongin, Gyeonggi Province. Known for its granite peaks and historical significance, featuring ancient fortress walls. The mountain serves as a natural boundary between Suwon and Yongin cities and is popular for hiking and outdoor activities.

9 Gukbap: A traditional Korean soup-and-rice dish where cooked rice is served in or with hot soup. Various types exist, including sundaeguk-bap (blood sausage soup with rice) and soegogi-gukbap (beef soup with rice). It's considered a hearty, affordable meal and is particularly popular for breakfast or as a hangover cure.

10 Jamsil Station: A major transportation hub in southeastern Seoul, adjacent to the Lotte World complex, Lotte World Tower, and Olympic Park. The area features major shopping centers, entertainment facilities, and serves as a central business district for the Gangnam area.

11 Gyeongbokgung: The largest and most important royal palace of the Joseon Dynasty, built in 1395. Located in northern Seoul, it served as the main royal palace and seat of power. Notable for its magnificent architecture, including Geunjeongjeon (throne hall) and Gyeonghoeru Pavilion. A prime example of traditional Korean palace architecture.

12 Sajik Park: A historic park next to Gyeongbokgung Palace, site of the Sajikdan Altar where kings of the Joseon Dynasty performed sacrificial rites to the gods of earth and grain. Today, it's a peaceful urban park featuring walking trails and recreational facilities.

13 Hwanghakjeong: A historic archery field located on Inwangsan Mountain, established in 1899 during the late Joseon Dynasty. One of Seoul's oldest traditional archery venues still in active use. The name means "Yellow Crane Pavilion," and it has been designated as Seoul's Tangible Cultural Property No. 25.

14 Tiger Statue: A stone tiger statue located on Inwangsan Mountain, different from the Tiger Rock. These tiger statues were traditionally placed as guardian figures in Korean culture, believed to ward off evil spirits and protect the area.

Made in the USA
Coppell, TX
16 November 2024

40364115R00144